MOTIVATION, EDUCATIONAL POLICY AND ACHIEVEMENT

Motivation, Educational Policy and Achievement seeks to theorise and critique current trends in education through the lens of key ideas from motivational theory. Its purpose is to argue that current educational trends on a macro level are a significant threat to the provision of classroom practices seeking to create an educational environment that, motivational theorists would argue, is best placed to develop motivational equality, optimal motivation and well-being.

Linking major contemporary theories of motivation to wider educational and political debate, this unique resource will bring about two major benefits: it will vocalise and mobilise the substantial research evidence from motivational theory in order to ensure that it contributes more explicitly to a critique of current neoliberal trends, and it will enable motivation researchers to be better positioned to move the theory forward in relation to what is happening in the real world of education. Areas covered include:

- developing a more critical space in relation to the field of motivational psychology and contemporary educational policy;
- linking motivational theory to education policy and broader social and political structures;
- the neoliberal educational landscape;
- an overview of achievement goal theory and self-determination theory.

Motivation, Educational Policy and Achievement is a 'wake-up call' for educational practitioners and policymakers and essential reading for all advanced students and researchers in the fields of educational psychology and educational research.

Sam Carr is a psychologist, a lecturer in education and the Director of Studies for Education with Psychology at the University of Bath, UK.

MOTIVATION, EDUCATIONAL POLICY AND ACHIEVEMENT

A critical perspective

Sam Carr

LONDON AND NEW YORK

First published 2016
by Routledge
2 Park Square, Milton Park, Abingdon, Oxon OX14 4RN

and by Routledge
711 Third Avenue, New York, NY 10017

Routledge is an imprint of the Taylor & Francis Group,
an informa business

© 2016 Sam Carr

The right of Sam Carr to be identified as author of this work has been asserted by him in accordance with sections 77 and 78 of the Copyright, Designs and Patents Act 1988.

All rights reserved. No part of this book may be reprinted or reproduced or utilised in any form or by any electronic, mechanical or other means, now known or hereafter invented, including photocopying and recording, or in any information storage or retrieval system, without permission in writing from the publishers.

Trademark notice: Product or corporate names may be trademarks or registered trademarks, and are used only for identification and explanation without intent to infringe.

British Library Cataloguing in Publication Data
A catalogue record for this book is available from the British Library

Library of Congress Cataloging in Publication Data
Names: Carr, Sam, 1977– author.
  Title: Motivation, educational policy, and achievement : a critical perspective / Sam Carr.Description: New York, NY : Routledge, 2016. | Includes bibliographical references.
  Identifiers: LCCN 2015023804| ISBN 9781138022089 (hbk) | ISBN 9781138022102 (pbk) | ISBN 9781315777245 (ebk)
  Subjects: LCSH: Education, Humanistic. | Motivation in education. | Education and state. | Neoliberalism.
  Classification: LCC LC1011 .C295 2016 | DDC 370.11/2–dc23
  LC record available at http://lccn.loc.gov/2015023804

ISBN: 978-1-138-02208-9 (hbk)
ISBN: 978-1-138-02210-2 (pbk)
ISBN: 978-1-315-77724-5 (ebk)

Typeset in Bembo
by Florence Production Ltd, Stoodleigh, Devon

CONTENTS

Acknowledgements vii

   Introduction 1

1 The neoliberal educational landscape 15

2 Creating a critical space 39

3 Discussing goal theory and contemporary educational policy 59

4 Discussing self-determination theory and contemporary educational policy 91

5 Some concluding thoughts 121

Index *135*

ACKNOWLEDGEMENTS

I would like to thank the following people for playing a part in helping me develop these ideas: (a) Dr Ceri Brown for spending many hours thoughtfully discussing my initial ideas and opening my eyes to the intersection between psychology, sociology and policy; (b) Ioannis Costas Batlle for some really helpful comments on early drafts and for many hours of conversation (in all manner of places) that have stimulated my thoughts and ideas no end; (c) Jenny Csecs for reading over early drafts, providing me with some helpful advice from a student perspective and taking an interest in the development of the ideas; (d) Alex, for being Alex and (e) Natalie May for support, for hours of thoughtful conversation and for inspiring me by helping me understand what it really means to passionately embrace and 'live' politics.

INTRODUCTION

This book is based upon the belief that education should authentically care for children and young people, striving to nurture, value and celebrate them for who they are, looking beyond their academic preparation and potential as knowledge workers and focusing upon their social, emotional, psychological, physical and spiritual needs as children and individuals. Like Nussbaum (2012), I argue that education ought to enable individuals to lead personally meaningful lives. However, it is difficult to contest the fact that educational policy has increasingly been incorporated into an agenda that views the construction of the knowledge worker as its *raison d'être* (Patrick, 2013). Ball (2003) has drawn attention to the fact that the reconstruction of education, in accordance with the language of the market, has both conjured and legitimised a whole new set of values, ethics and codes of practice among education providers, teachers and students. Increasingly, non-market values have been devalued, replaced by 'the "need" to "sell" schools and colleges and make and manage image in the competitive education marketplace' (Ball, 2003, p. 31). Not only does this market ontology 'teach and disseminate a new morality' (Ball, 2003, p. 31), but it also serves to restructure the ways in which we 'think ourselves' and 'the criteria and norms we use to judge ourselves' (Rose, 1992, p. 161).

Clearly, what constitutes social justice is always contested, fluctuating according to time and space, and changeable, dependent upon historical juncture, social group or spatial location (Vincent, 2003). It is far beyond the scope of this book to offer an exhaustive explication of social justice. However, it is worth briefly setting out some of the critical principles forwarded by key theorists (Miller, 2003; Rawls, 2003).

For Rawls (2003), social justice is about ensuring and protecting equal access to liberties, rights and opportunities, as well as caring for the least advantaged people in a society. From this perspective, whether something is just or unjust depends upon whether it advances or impedes equality of access to important civil liberties, human rights and opportunities for healthy and fulfilling lives, as well as whether it allocates a fair share of benefits to the least advantaged people in society. Similarly, Miller (2003) views social justice as predominantly concerned with the distribution of advantages and disadvantages in society (and with how these things *should* be distributed). He highlights:

> When we attack some policy or some state of affairs as socially unjust, we are claiming that a person, or more usually a category of persons, enjoys fewer advantages than that person or group of persons ought to enjoy (or bears more of the burdens than they ought to bear), given how other members of the society in question are fairing. (Miller, 2003, p. 1)

When Rawls (2003) and Miller (2003) write of the least advantaged members of society, they are referring to those who lack basic advantages such as money, property, jobs, education, healthcare, childcare, care for the elderly, personal security, housing, transportation or leisure. For Rawls (2003), these advantages are 'things citizens need as free and equal persons living a complete life; they are not things it is simply rational to want or desire, or to prefer or even to crave' (Rawls, 2003, p. 58). Rawls (2003, pp. 58–59) considered the following as advantages:

- basic rights and liberties: freedom of thought and liberty of conscience;
- freedom of movement and free choice of occupation against a background of diverse opportunities that allow the pursuit of a variety of ends and give effect to decisions to revise and alter them;
- powers and prerogatives of office and position of authority and responsibility;
- income and wealth generally needed to achieve a wide range of ends, whatever they may be;
- the social platform for the development of self-respect, understood as those aspects of basic institutions normally essential if citizens are to have a lively sense of their worth as persons and to be able to advance their ends with self-confidence.

The material in this book is particularly concerned with the last point, the idea that social justice also involves interrogating the extent to which social structures and institutions provide a platform for equal access to psychological goods such as self-respect and a sense of worth and value.

What is more, other theorists have also noted that the least advantaged members of society also suffer from an unfair allocation of *disadvantages*, which may refer to factors such as military service, dangerous work, unemployment and all manner of other hardships (Miller, 2003). Miller (2003) noted that when considering how various policies and institutions allocate advantages and disadvantages, it is not necessarily the case that we should evaluate them based upon how they benefit us personally. He argued:

> Justice is about assigning benefits whose values are established by their worth to the relevant population taken as a whole, and it must be blind to personal preferences . . . justice fundamentally requires us to treat people as equals . . . we should understand justice as what people would agree to in advance of knowing their own stake in the decision to be reached. Social justice efforts can not merely be rationalizations of self-interest. (Miller, 2003, p. 87)

It is becoming increasingly difficult to contest the fact that neoliberal logic has disrupted social justice in a myriad of ways. As Brodie (2007, p. 93) outlines:

> The neoliberal project has taken on many different configurations across national settings. Everywhere, however, this mode of governance has concentrated incomes and wealth among a few, squeezed the middle income strata, and fuelled unparalleled inequalities in income wealth, and life chances. If there is one consistent indicator of neoliberal governance, it is stalled, if not declining human development and well-being amidst unprecedented economic growth and wealth creation. It is a governing formula that is ripe with all manner of social injustices.

In this book, I echo Brodie's (2007) sentiment and contend that in neoliberal society there are compelling reasons to place social justice at the heart of social science inquiry. Accordingly, the British Educational Research Association's (BERA) Special Interest Group (SIG) in Social Justice has suggested that academic critique in education must take every opportunity to influence and challenge political agendas that impede social justice (Vincent, 2003).

This book specifically focuses upon the interface between social justice, the neoliberal educational landscape and motivational psychology. Clearly, education is a social institution that has a significant impact upon whether people are able to 'locate' a sense of their worth as persons and to advance their ends with self-confidence and respect. In order to do this, education must inspire, enthuse and help meet young people's social, emotional, psychological, physical and spiritual needs – it should empower and support change and personal development from within (Ryan and Weinstein, 2009). Over thirty years ago, Nicholls and Burton (1982) wrote a paper called 'Motivation and Equality'. They stated:

> We start with the assumption that all students should develop their capacities to the fullest possible extent (Dewey, 1938/1963). If they did, we would have an acceptable form of equality in education. Individuals would be unequal in achievement but equal in the extent to which they had attained their potential. Equal educational achievement is not desirable because it would mean inequality of fulfillment of potential. (p. 367)

Furthermore, Nicholls and Burton (1982) highlighted that educational goals such as equality in relation to the fulfilment of potential are simply unattainable if attention is not paid to equality in relation to the establishment and maintenance of students' absorption in and motivation towards education. Almost all educational objectives are dependent for their attainment on this simple precondition and a socially just society, where education is available, enriching, empowering and self-worth-enhancing for all citizens ought to position motivation as an educational priority. As Deci, Vallerand, Pelletier and Ryan (1991, p. 325) noted:

> In their formative first two decades, individuals spend about 15,000 hrs in schools. Thus schools represent a primary socializing influence that has enormous impact on the course of people's lives and, in turn, on society. Ideal school systems are ones that succeed in promoting in students a genuine enthusiasm for learning and accomplishment and a sense of volitional involvement in the educational enterprise.

Nonetheless, in the last thirty years, we have witnessed a political transformation of education into a system that views children and young people as knowledge workers, to be 'produced', to 'perform' and 'held accountable' to the needs of the market (Ball, 2003; Giroux, 2002; Patrick, 2013). It is critical to reflect upon whether such a transformation is directing us towards the sort of motivational equality and enthusiasm for learning discussed above. Almost a quarter of a century ago, in the educational psychology literature, Deci et al. (1991, pp. 341–342) stated:

> Classrooms are embedded in schools; schools are embedded in communities and society. From our perspective, the extent to which the school context is more autonomy supportive, rather than controlling, will directly affect the extent to which teachers support the autonomy of their students. This issue, with its many ramifications, needs much further work . . . the rhetoric from Washington continues to advocate greater accountability, greater discipline, and increased use of standardized testing, all of which are means of exerting greater pressure and control on the educational process and therefore are likely to have at least some negative consequences.

There are a myriad of reasons to suggest (a) that neoliberal educational policy has been ill-considered in relation to human motivation and well-being and (b) that (despite rallying calls such as Deci et al.'s) motivational psychology has been surprisingly muted in relation to challenging and influencing such policy. In the spirit of the BERA Social Justice SIG's call, my intention in this book is to further mobilise the field of motivational psychology towards challenging and influencing this agenda.

Mary's story

Some years ago I was reminded of how injustice can be unwittingly fostered by educational policy when I conducted a series of retrospective interviews (as part of a broader research project) with Mary, a sixty-one-year-old divorcee in the UK.

Our interviews focused upon her experiences of the eleven-plus examination in 1958. In short, following the Second World War, the 1944 Education Act sought to reform the provision of secondary education in England and Wales. Based upon the outcome of a rigid, end-of-primary 'intelligence' test (Brine, 2006; Chitty, 1997), children were channelled towards either a grammar school education *or* education in a technical or secondary modern school. The system of selection was heavily based upon psychologists' (Burt, 1959) belief that each child possessed an innate, unalterable intelligence that dictated their suitability for either an academic, technical or functional secondary education. The eleven-plus examination determined whether children were best suited to a more academic secondary education route within the grammar school system (preparing them for A-levels and potential university entrance), or to a more functional, technical education within the secondary modern and technical school systems.

Brine (2006) has highlighted how, for many children, the eleven-plus was an educational experience that played a pivotal role in their lives and in the construction of key aspects of their character and identity. She suggests, '. . . it was the pivotal point of selection; a key moment in constructing the dispositions of children as either bright and successful or "thick" and a failure' (Brine, 2006, p. 43). Mary's story particularly illuminates this suggestion. Below, with her permission, I offer a brief extract from her biographical interview.

> Something definitely changed at about 7 or 8 years old. My brother was involved in this eleven-plus thing and I heard all the talking about it. That's when it became something in my head too. I realised that this horrible thing was going to happen *to me too*! I saw that my brother hated it. For some reason *I* was getting nervous watching *him* go through this eleven-plus thing. But he passed. I saw how great that was to Dad and I'd got all that to go through myself!
>
> The eleven-plus meant, or at least *Dad* had made it mean, absolutely everything. He always said, 'Oh, you'll walk through that'. He thought it was so important in life and he didn't realise how unhappy and worried it made me. I had it ingrained in my head that entry into Grammar School was the best thing, no, the only thing to do, if you wanted to do well. At one stage it seemed as though that was all they ever talked about. Apparently it meant that you were supposedly clever, intelligent . . . yeah . . . and passing the eleven-plus *made* you intelligent and successful . . . and if you failed you were no good.
>
> You know, I always thought I was *good* at Maths and writing and that. I would never go home thinking 'God I can't do that'. But then, almost overnight, I felt like a complete and total failure. I felt like I was no good at anything. And that all started with my eleven-plus. Do you know . . . I can't even remember *taking* the eleven-plus. But I can remember the day the letter came and I hadn't passed. I can remember the letter arriving. I can remember running down to the bottom of the garden, crying my eyes out

and hiding. Why? Because I felt like shit and I didn't want to see anyone. I felt a total failure. I remember the thing coming in the post and opening it, or Dad opening it, saying something like 'you've not been successful, errr . . . I'll look into this' and I just ran away. I was thinking how I'd let everybody down, how I didn't meet requirements as a daughter or as a person. I just wanted to run away because I felt so upset.

It was such a big kick in the teeth because I thought it was very important. Deep down I suppose *I thought* Dad didn't love me because of it. I'm sure he did but that's what I thought. I felt less of a person too. This was all they ever talked about. It was always just thrown at me . . . and it was a *shock* . . . it was a *shock* to him, the school, and me that I didn't make it. I was always scared that I would never measure up to expectations and now I knew that I didn't, I knew that I wasn't that 'clever, capable child'.

After I failed they let me go to an interview, for the eleven-plus. Dad had 'specially arranged' it because he was a teacher and he knew people in the right places. It was like a second chance to pass the eleven-plus. He should never have done that. In the end it meant I failed twice and it was a big enough thing for me just once. But I was pleased because I thought 'oooh great I'm going to be doing something right'! I had to go in, spend fifteen minutes to half an hour with the Headmaster and someone else and they asked me questions. I can remember one of the questions that I got wrong. They asked me what a 'Saddleback' was. It was a pig but I didn't know it was a pig so I got that wrong. But I've known ever since.

Then I found out that result . . . a failure still. I felt my self-esteem had reached zero. And did I get over it? I don't think I did. I never got over it. I'm sorry but I'm going to cry in a minute. I'm sorry . . . just give me a minute (*Mary pauses . . . cries . . . composes herself . . . and continues*).

I think it affected me for the rest of my life, the fact that I was second best. I was 'injured' in it. I think I never again trusted, no that's not the right word, I never again allowed myself to believe and, before that, I *did* believe, that I was going to be successful. I wasn't going to *try* to go to university and I wasn't going to *try* to do this or that again because I was frightened of that awful feeling again. And that's gone through life. Jobs for example, I can do jobs well but I've never wanted to strive for more because I felt I wasn't capable of it.

Mary's sad story is simply an illustration, an example of why we ought to more carefully interrogate the interface between psychological theory, educational policy, and the broader political ends such policy so frequently serves. As Bartky (1990) has noted, when we think about people as 'oppressed' we most often have something political or economic in mind. However, we must remember that people *can* be oppressed psychologically. In fact, a key feature of oppression is always its psychological internalisation. For Bartky (1990, p. 22):

> To be psychologically oppressed is to be weighed down in your mind; it is to have a harsh dominion exercised over your self-esteem. The psychologically oppressed become their own oppressors; they come to exercise dominion over their own self-esteem. Differently put, psychological oppression can be regarded as the 'internalization of intimations of inferiority'.

Her words closely reflect Paulo Freire's ideas about oppression, reflecting an acute awareness of the ways in which people internalise oppressive discourse and turn it upon themselves:

> Self-depreciation is another characteristic of the oppressed, which derives from their internalization of the opinion the oppressors hold of them. So often do they hear that they are good for nothing, know nothing and are incapable of learning anything – that they are sick, lazy, and unproductive – that in the end they become convinced of their own unfitness. (Freire, 1970, p. 63)

As a researcher who has devoted much of my life to exploring, understanding and researching human motivation, Mary's story brings alive some of the key ideas and constructs that have been central to contemporary theories of motivation, and raises questions about how they are inextricably tied to oppression in educational life.

For example, the narrative depicts a child, family and education system caught up in the lay belief that children's intelligence is a fixed, unalterable entity (Dweck, 2000), provoking a concern about how much of this 'fixed intelligence' the child possesses and arousing concern that the intelligence she has been rationed will be good enough (or not). In the motivational literature, it is well documented that experiences of failure framed within such a theory of ability (and normative standards of success) can have devastating effects on perceptions of the self and subsequent emotional and behavioural responses (Molden and Dweck, 2006). Smiley and Dweck (1994) suggest that when faced with failure, children who view educational tasks as an indicator of the amount of intelligence or ability they possess inaccurately underestimate past performances and expect poor performance in the future. Furthermore, the low perceptions of competence that often accompany such failure experiences ensure that individuals are more sensitive to future possibilities of failure (Elliot, 1997, 1999). Hence, they are perhaps more likely to focus themselves on perpetually avoiding the negative consequence of inferiority.

Critical educational psychologists (Claiborne, 2014) have highlighted the potential significance that ideas and constructs from motivational theory (such as Dweck's ideas discussed above) could hold in relation to challenging implicit assumptions upon which (potentially) psychologically oppressive educational policy is grounded. For example, Claiborne (2014, p. 4) highlights how Dweck's ideas could provide a strong theoretical basis for challenging and transforming assumptions 'that are consistent with meritocratic views of society, based on the notion of a humankind distributed into a fixed hierarchy of worth based on bodily capacities'. She has also noted, however, that while Dweck's ideas clearly hold the potential to 'rattle the cage' of normative practice, they have never been fully recognised in a wider political context, despite their potential to disrupt dominant 'essentialist assumptions about human bodies and knowable selves' (Claiborne, 2014, p. 5).

From another perspective, Ryan and Deci (2006) have noted the enormous importance of the need for relatedness in relation to human motivation in the context of self-determination theory. They have outlined that people are highly motivated to be recognised and loved by others, yet, as Mary's story depicts, parents, teachers and peers often make their affection or regard contingent upon children meeting specific expectations or sharing their views. Clearly, such a need for relatedness threatens to be undermined by policies that communicate to individuals, teachers and schools that they are positively regarded *if* they are able to learn, achieve or behave according to a particular prescription. Assor, Roth and Deci (2004) have viewed this sort of 'conditional regard' in education as a form of control or manipulation and have identified that use of conditional regard tends to result in more fragile self-esteem, transient satisfaction following successes, greater shame following failure and feelings of rejection by and resentment towards their controlling agents such as parents or teachers.

An important point to consider in Mary's story is the connection between her psychological experiences on an individual level and broader discourse created by educational policy (and, as some have argued, informed by knowledge construction from educational psychology). That is, her story is played out upon a policy platform that might be seen to have contributed to the preconditions for psychological oppression. Specifically, the eleven-plus reflected the political position that '... schools should not be thought of as providing an enriching and creative environment, but should be adjusted to the function of sorting out and selecting the "bright" from the "dull", as determined by nature' (Lawler, 1978, p. 3). This belief had filtered down from psychologists, to government, to schools, and was, unsurprisingly, internalised by families and children themselves (Chitty, 1997).

Ultimately, Mary's story is a reminder that educational policy plays a role in sculpting critical features of the landscape in which children are asked to learn, setting the parameters within which their psychological experiences and educational narrative unfold and play out. We must also remember that her story is about power too. As Foucault (1997, pp. 291–292) noted, 'power is always present: I mean a relationship in which one person tries to control the conduct of the other'. In his discussion of power, Prilleltensky (2008) suggested that power is, on the one hand, about the opportunity and capacity for people to fulfil or obstruct personal and collective needs. But he noted that it is about oppression too – and regardless of motives, some people, groups or institutions *do* oppress others. Such oppression can be directed inwards, towards the self or towards family members and others in the context of institutions or broader communities.

Prilleltensky (2008, p. 121) noted that 'power can be used to resist oppression and pursue liberation'. In the interests of social justice, a key premise behind this book is the need to develop a critical space in psychological theory that seeks to utilise our own power by exploring the interface between the knowledge we construct and educational policy. As Brine (2006) has outlined, the bilateral schooling system and its classification system of grammar and modern schools (which reproduced implicit class-, ability-, and gender-related value structures) were literally internalised and manifested in the dispositions of children and young people. Despite its obvious shortcomings, this oppressive social and political policy was not resisted strongly enough by academic disciplines such as psychology, and they may even have played their part in creating it (Brine, 2006). To ensure that we learn our lessons in the context of our modern political struggles, I believe it is essential we develop and maintain an active critical consciousness.

Neoliberal educational policy and a critical psychological space

However it is defined, psychology has consistently been guilty of failing to prioritise social and political justice (Louis *et al.*, 2014); critics have, for some time, lamented the discipline's *social amnesia* (Prilleltensky and Walsh-Bowers, 1993), *moral inertia* (Maxwell, 1991) and *moral shyness* (Prilleltensky, 1997). There have been concerns (Burman, 2008; Carr and Batlle, 2015; Louis *et al.*, 2014; Sugarman, 2015) that without a strong critical conscience, research and knowledge in psychology might simply be incorporated into the neoliberal educational project, risking, as Rose (1990, p. 93) has warned, becoming the science of the calculable child, 'whose individuality is no longer ineffable, unique and beyond knowledge, but can be known, mapped, calibrated, evaluated, quantified, predicted and managed'.

As Parker (2009) has asserted, political struggles outside of psychology have often provoked the emergence of small pockets of critical or theoretical psychological thought that has been either explicitly activist in nature, or has assimilated political debate into its own conceptual and methodological discussions (Rose, 1990, 1985). In the same tradition, this book has been written to stimulate critical reflection among fellow scholars and students of psychology about the possibility of creating a more critical, politically aware space in the field of human motivation, developing and nurturing a social conscience that might be more clearly reflected in the knowledge we construct, the questions we ask and the ends to which our theories are developed to serve.

As Fowers (2015) has noted, theoretical and critical psychology's most significant functions involve (a) researching and reflecting upon psychological theories, research and practice; (b) re-examining and critically questioning blind spots, assumptions, methods and interpretations and (c) reformulating and redirecting theory, research and practice on the back of such reflection and critique. In his outline of theoretical psychology's *raison d'être*, Fowers (2015, p. 5) has suggested:

> As theoretical psychologists, we have developed powerful critical tools to reveal and analyze the blind spots, ideologies, unacknowledged moral commitments, and overstated objectivism in psychology. These tools and the critiques they potentiate are invaluable contributions to the discipline. There

is no possibility of becoming a reflective, progressive discipline without this kind of reflection and critique. These critiques are not generally welcomed with open arms, but we can increase receptivity to our work by attending carefully and understanding charitably our colleagues' aims and concerns. We accomplish this by carefully and thoroughly researching the work on which we are reflecting.

In relation to neoliberalism, a critical approach to psychological inquiry operates from a position that rationalises the refusal of oppressive ideology, illuminates the plight of those who suffer because of it and aims for disciplinary transformation that places social justice at the heart of conceptual and methodological developments (Carr and Batlle, 2015; Parker, 2009). By such criteria, the development of a political conscience necessitates that researchers give serious contemplation to how (and whether) their specific theories might be seen to serve, facilitate or resist a given political stance.

Psychological theory in and of itself may be *portrayed* as 'value-neutral'. However, research and practice invariably (even when it is not made explicit) have implications for political and social justice and can unwittingly serve as an instrument of oppression (Carr and Batlle, 2015; Louis *et al.*, 2014). One does not have to look very far to substantiate such claims. For example, in recent decades it has been argued that a cultural and political context loaded with anxieties surrounding control of unruly children and an education system in which teachers, parents and children are pressured towards viewing non-conformity to a myopic set of learning practices and behavioural norms as 'pathological', has provided the perfect social platform for the normalisation of concepts such as ADHD within psychology and beyond (Timimi, 2002). Critical perspectives on psychology's role in the 'medicalisation of childhood' (Rafalovich, 2013) have made a compelling case for drawing attention to a correlation between political mandates within educational policy and rates of diagnosis for such disorders (Fulton *et al.*, 2009).

As Louis *et al.* (2014) have highlighted, the emergence of new groups, identities and voices (in psychology on the whole or at the micro-level, within sub-disciplines or individual theories themselves) with differing agendas, assumptions, values and codes need not *replace* 'what is'. However, it is important to realise that only through the emergence of new groups and voices are we able to bring to light particular values (e.g. social justice, political conscience) that may have previously been marginal or confined to 'zones of indifference' within the codes of practice of dominant groups. Accordingly, as the norms and values of existing and emerging voices are contested and conflicted, individuals, subgroups and groups are challenged to position themselves in relation to such norms and values (Louis, 2008).

The emergence of spaces and voices that prioritise social justice in relation to psychological thought and inquiry is something that might be offered more generally, as a guiding framework or ideal for the discipline on a broader, macro level (Fowers, 2015; Louis *et al.*, 2014). However, I contend that it is also something that can (and should) happen on a micro level, with emerging voices within individual sub-disciplines and theories seeking to reflect upon, re-examine and reformulate their language, discourse and agenda so that it might better prioritise and be mindful of social justice (Carr and Batlle, 2015). In this book, I intend to stimulate debate, reflection and critical thought in relation to how some of the dominant theories of human motivation in the context of education might develop in a climate where educational policy increasingly reflects the agenda of a political establishment seeking to position education as, above all else, an instrument of economic prosperity (Hursh, 2007). The book is written in the spirit of Fowers's (2015) call to reflect upon, re-examine and begin to reformulate an alternative space within the motivational psychology of education that places social justice and political conscience higher up its agenda.

In the following chapter (Chapter 1 – The neoliberal educational landscape), I sketch out for readers some of the key features of the neoliberal educational landscape and discuss how education has been transformed by the neoliberal agenda. In Chapter 2 (Creating a critical space), I outline the need for psychological knowledge to carefully consider its role and ethical obligations as a critical conscience against a neoliberal educational backdrop. This chapter ends by outlining the usefulness of thinking about such a critical space in the context of contemporary theories of educational motivation. Subsequently, in Chapters 3 and 4 (Discussing goal theory and contemporary educational policy and Discussing self-determination theory and contemporary educational policy), I seek to critically explore the interface between educational policy and two theories (goal theory and self-determination) that have been central to the educational motivation literature. In the spirit of Fowers's (2015) call, these chapters discuss the ways in which the knowledge generated by such theories relates to educational policy, the ways in which these bodies of knowledge might be used to critique aspects of policy and the possibility for future research that is located in a concern for social justice and real world awareness. Finally, in Chapter 5 (Some concluding thoughts), I discuss some of the significant questions and issues for us to consider as we move forward and seek to create a genuinely critical space in motivational theory that prioritises social justice in the context of educational policy.

References

Assor, A., Roth, G., and Deci, E.L. (2004). The emotional costs of parents' conditional regard: A self-determination theory analysis. *Journal of Personality*, 72(1), 47–88.

Ball, S. (2003). Social justice in the head: Are we all libertarians now? In C. Vincent (ed.), *Social Justice, Education, and Identity* (pp. 31–50). London: Routledge Falmer.

Bartky, S.L. (1990). *Femininity and domination: Studies in the phenomenology of domination*. New York: Routledge.

Brine, J. (2006). The everyday classificatory practices of selective schooling: A fifty year retrospective study. *International Studies in Sociology of Education*, 16(1), 35–52.

Brodie, J. (2007). Reforming social justice in neoliberal times. *Studies in Social Justice*, 1, 93–107.

Burman, E. (2008). *Deconstructing Developmental Psychology*. London: Brunner-Routledge.

Burt, C. (1959). The evidence for the concept of intelligence. In S. Wiseman (ed.), *Intelligence and Ability*. Harmondsworth: Penguin.
Carr, S. and Batlle, I.C. (2015). Attachment theory, neoliberalism, and social conscience. *Journal of Theoretical and Philosophical Psychology*, *35*(3), 160–76.
Chitty, C. (1997). The school effectiveness movement: Origins, shortcomings and future possibilities. *The Curriculum Journal*, *8*(1), 45–62.
Claiborne, L. (2014). The potential of critical educational psychology beyond its meritocratic past. In T. Corcoran (ed.), *Psychology in Education: Critical Theory~Practice* (pp. 1–11). Rotterdam: Sense.
Deci, E.L., Vallerand, R.J., Pelletier, L.G., and Ryan, R.M. (1991). Motivation and Education: The Self-Determination Perspective. *Educational Psychologist*, *26*(3), 325–346.
Dewey, J. (1938/1963). *Education and Experience*. New York: Collier.
Dweck, C.S. (2000). *Self-theories: Their role in motivation, personality and development*. Philadelphia, PA: Taylor & Francis.
Elliot, A.J. (1997). Integrating the "classic" and "contemporary" approaches to achievement motivation: A hierarchical model of approach and avoidance achievement motivation. In M.L. Maehr and P.R. Pintrich (eds), *Advances in Motivation and Achievement* (Vol. 10, pp. 143–179). Greenwich, CT: JAI Press.
Elliot, A.J. (1999). Approach and avoidance motivation and achievement goals. *Educational Psychologist*, *34*(3), 169–89.
Foucault, M. (1997). The ethics of the concern of the self as a practice of freedom. In P. Rabinow (ed.), *Michel Foucault: Ethics, Subjectivity and Truth* (pp. 281–301). New York: The New Press.
Fowers, B.J. (2015). The promise of a flourishing theoretical psychology. *Journal of Theoretical and Philosophical Psychology*, 35(3), 145–589Online First, 2013.
Fulton, B.D., Scheffler, R.M., Hinshaw, S.P., Levine, P., Stone, S., Brown, T.T., and Modrek, S. (2009). National variation of ADHD diagnostic prevalence and medication use: Health care providers and education policies. *Psychiatric Services*, *60*(8), 1075–83.
Giroux, H.A. (2002). Neoliberalism, corporate culture, and the promise of higher education: The university as a democratic public sphere. *Harvard Educational Review*, 72, 425–63.
Hirsch, D. (September 2007). *Experiences of Poverty and Educational Disadvantage*. York, UK: Joseph Rowntree Foundation. Available at www.jrf.org.uk/knowledge/findings/socialpolicy/2123.asp [Accessed 5 January 2015].
Lawler, J.M. (1978). *IQ, Heritability and Racism: A Marxist Critique of ensenism*. London: Lawrence and Wishart.
Louis, W.R. (2008). Intergroup positioning and power. In F. M. Moghaddam, R. Harré, and N. Lee (eds), *Global Conflict Resolution Through Positioning Analysis* (pp. 21–39). New York, NY: Springer.
Louis, W.R., Mavor, K.I., La Macchia, S.T. and Amiot, C.E. (2014). Social justice and psychology: What is, and what should be. *Journal of Theoretical and Philosophical Psychology*, *34*(1), 14–27.
Maxwell, M. (1991). *Moral inertia*. Niwot, CO: University of Colorado Press.
Miller, D. (2003). *Principles of Social Justice*. Boston, MA: Harvard University Press.
Molden, D.C., and Dweck, C.S. (2006). Finding "meaning" in psychology: A lay theories approach to self-regulation, social perception, and social development. *American Psychologist*, *61*(3), 192–203.
Nicholls, J.G. and Burton, J.T. (1982). Motivation and equality. *Elementary School Journal*, *82*(4), 67–78.
Nussbaum, M. (2012). *Not for Profit: Why Democracy Needs the Humanities*. Princeton, NJ: Princeton University Press.

Parker, I. (2009). Critical Psychology and Revolutionary Marxism. *Theory & Psychology*, *19*(1), 71–92.

Patrick, F. (2013). Neoliberalism, the knowledge economy, and the learner: Challenging the inevitability of the commodified self as an outcome of education. *International Scholarly Research Network: Education*, *2013*, 8.

Prilleltensky, I. (1997). Values, assumptions, and practices: Assessing the moral implications of psychological discourse and action. *American Psychologist*, *52*(5), 517–35.

Prilleltensky, I. (2008). The role of power in wellness, oppression, and liberation: The promise of psychopolitical validity. *Journal of Community Psychology*, *36*(2), 116–36.

Prilleltensky, I., and Walsh-Bowers, R. (1993). Psychology and the moral imperative. *Journal of Theoretical and Philosophical Psychology*, *13*(2), 90–102.

Rafalovich, A. (2013). Attention deficit-hyperactivity Disorder as the medicalisation of childhood: Challenges from and for sociology. *Sociology compass*, *7*(5), 343–54.

Rawls, J. (2003). *Justice as Fairness: A Restatement* (2nd edn). Boston, MA: Belknap Press.

Rose, N. (1985). *The Psychological Complex: Psychology, Politics and Society in England 1869–1939*. London: Routledge and Kegan Paul.

Rose, N. (1990). *Governing the Soul: The Shaping of the Private Self*. London: Routledge.

Rose, N. (1992). Governing the enterprising self. In P. Heelas and P. Morris (eds), *The Values of the Enterprise Culture*. London: Routledge.

Ryan, R.M., and Deci, E.L. (2006). Self-determination and the problem of human autonomy: Does psychology need choice, self-determination and will? *Journal of Personality*, *74*, 1557–86.

Ryan, R.M. and Weinstein, N. (2009). A self-determination theory perspective on high-stakes testing. *Theory and Research in Education*, *7*(2), 224–33.

Smiley, P.A., and Dweck, C.S. (1994). Individual differences in achievement goals among young children. *Child Development*, *65*(6), 1723–43.

Sugarman, J. (2015). Neoliberalism and psychological ethics. *Journal of Theoretical and Philosophical Psychology*, *35*, 103–116.

Timimi, S. (2002). *Pathological Child Psychiatry and the Medicalization of Childhood*. London, UK: Brunner-Routledge.

Vincent, C. (2003). Introduction. In C. Vincent (ed.), *Social Justice, Education, and Identity*. London: Routledge Falmer.

1
THE NEOLIBERAL EDUCATIONAL LANDSCAPE

> An ideological position can never be really successful until it is naturalized, and it cannot be naturalized while it is still thought of as a value rather than a fact. Accordingly, neoliberalism has sought to eliminate the very category of value in the ethical sense. Over the past thirty years, capitalist realism has successfully installed a 'business ontology' in which it is 'simply obvious' that everything in society, including healthcare and education, should be run as a business. . . . [E]mancipatory politics must always destroy the appearance of a 'natural order', must reveal what is presented as 'necessary and inevitable' to be a mere contingency, just as it must make what was previously deemed to be impossible seem attainable.
>
> (Fisher, 2009, p. 16)

The age of neoliberalism

The concept of neoliberalism has, during the past twenty years or so, been popular in political and academic debate, and it is common for authors to suggest that we currently live in the 'neoliberal society' or the 'age of neoliberalism' (Thorsen and Lie, 2006). However, the popularity of the term does not imply that it is a clearly defined concept (Thorsen, 2010). Given the myriad of authors who have failed to outline their interpretation of neoliberalism and the almost exclusive appropriation of the term by critics (self-proclaimed neoliberals are a rare breed), the outcome has been the frequent reduction of neoliberalism to a synonym for 'any negative effect caused by the free market' (Boas and Gans-Morse, 2009; Thorsen, 2010).

Attempts to clarify the term (Barnett, 2010; Harvey, 2005; Thorsen, 2010) have centred particularly upon the idea that neoliberalism reflects a family of ideas and political beliefs associated with the revival of economic liberalism (taken to include the ideas of thinkers such as Friedrich von Hayek and Joseph Schumpeter of the school of Austrian economics and Milton Friedman of the 'Chicago School' of economics) in the mid-twentieth century. Authors (Read, 2009) have distinguished *neoliberalism* from what has been termed *classical liberalism* (Locke, 1689; Smith, 1776) on the basis of specific features of economic activity. In classical liberalism, economic activity is principally focused upon in terms of the exchange of private property and distribution of goods. From this perspective, classical liberalism naturalises the market 'as a system with its own rationality, its own interest, and its own specific efficiency, arguing ultimately for its superior efficiency as a distributor of goods and services' (Read, 2009, p. 27). Most importantly, under classical liberalism, the market is a space within which individuals are autonomous in their acts of exchange, and it is assumed that this space must be safeguarded by the state, enacting laws that protect individuals' unconditional right to private property and market-based liberty. As Read (2009) has noted, classical liberalism makes *exchange* the general organising force for society. However, neoliberalism, according to Foucault (2008), represents an evolved, extended version of the idea that economic activity and exchange should serve as an organising social and political force. In neoliberalism, the right to exchange is preserved, *but* what is added is an emphasis on the necessity for competition. For Read (2009, p. 28), what is most important to note about the shift from classical liberalism to neoliberalism is:

> this shift in 'anthropology' from 'homo-economicus' as an *exchanging* creature to a *competitive* creature, or rather as a creature whose tendency to compete must be fostered, entails a general shift in the way in which human beings make themselves and are made subjects.

Of course, like classical liberalism, neoliberalism holds that the only legitimate purpose of the state is to safeguard individual (especially commercial) liberty and strong private property rights (Hayek, 1979; Nozick, 1974). There has also been the belief that the state should possess minimal (or at least drastically reduced) power, strength and size, and that any transgression by the state beyond this sole, legitimate purpose (i.e. protecting individual liberty, market freedom and a competitive playing field) is unacceptable (Thorsen, 2010). Harvey's (2005, p. 2) definition summarises:

> Neoliberalism is in the first instance a theory of political economic practices that proposes that human well-being can best be advanced by liberating individual entrepreneurial freedoms and skills within an institutional framework characterized by strong private property rights, free markets and free trade. The role of the state is to create and preserve an institutional framework appropriate to such practices. The state has to guarantee, for example, the quality and integrity of money. It must also set up those military, defence, police and legal structures and functions required to secure private property rights and to guarantee, by force if need be, the proper functioning of markets. Furthermore, if markets do not exist (in areas such as land, water, education, health care, social security, or environmental pollution) then they must be created, by state action if necessary. But beyond these tasks the state

should not venture. State interventions in markets (once created) must be kept to a bare minimum because, according to the theory, the state cannot possibly possess enough information to second-guess market signals (prices) and because powerful interest groups will inevitably distort and bias state interventions (particularly in democracies) for their own benefit.

This definition positions neoliberalism as an economic-political paradigm. However, Larner (2000, 2006) has outlined that it has also been thought of as a hegemonic ideology and a distinctive form of governmentality. For example, as Thorsen and Lie (2006, p. 14) have asserted, 'free markets and free trade will, it is believed, set free the creative potential and the entrepreneurial spirit which is built into the spontaneous order of any human society, and thereby lead to more individual liberty and well-being, and a more efficient allocation of resources'. Neoliberal ideology then, in line with the aforementioned free market values, staunchly upholds individual freedom and responsibility (Larner, 2000). Akin to how the State should refrain from imposing constraints on the market, government should not hamper citizens' freedom by inflicting on them the burdens of the welfare state (spending on social support and equality of opportunity – see Briggs, 1961, for a review). Margaret Thatcher (1987, p. 10) popularly encapsulated this notion when she claimed, 'there is no such thing as society, there are individual men and women and there are families'. Responsibility, according to neoliberal discourse, is conceptualised in terms of subscribing to the free market's values (Brown, 2003): survival of the fittest as determined by the accumulation of wealth in a competitive society, endorsing 'ruthless competitive individualism' to achieve one's goals (Giroux, 2005, p. 8). Those individuals who deviate from this model are chastised for their failure to embrace personal agency and improve the financial, health or educational components of their lives (Coakley, 2011; Kendall, 2003). There is limited scope to appreciate that a person's current situation is shaped by factors beyond individual choice, such as the amount of opportunities available to them, the quality of the opportunities and the environment in which they become available. Consequently, for example, it has been suggested that neoliberal rhetoric rationalises poverty one-dimensionally, as a personal failure to embrace the work ethic required to climb out of despondency (Harvey, 2007).

Of particular concern for critics is the idea that neoliberal values ever more pervasively shape and hijack everyday life, transforming practice in a number of social, cultural and institutional fields. Heynon, McCarthy, Prudham and Robbins (2007) have noted that there has been significant empirical work on the way in which neoliberal policy has been circulated, defined as a lofty panacea, slippery and difficult to justify as the basis for policy formation in a myriad of contexts, yet with entirely concrete and drastic effects on the lived experiences of people. The following section discusses some of the key features of the transformation of education under neoliberal society and explores the ways in which the literature has critiqued its effects.

Knowledge capitalism and education

In his description of the 'crisis' currently facing contemporary youth, Giroux (2003) outlines how a central principle of modernity has been the idea that youth embody a society's hopes and dreams for its future. At the heart of democracy there has been an implicit expectation that governments and political systems would value, prioritise and safeguard the resources, social provision and education system necessary to nurture young people's future and the future of democracy. This reflects the fact that we are committed to and believe in fighting for the rights of our children, developing policy that genuinely prioritises their future and offering them an educational platform that helps them to become critical citizens and simultaneously enhances their inner life. Clearly, educational provision is the ultimate reflection of a society's commitment to youth and future democracy. In educational policy and practice, we are able to glimpse how we currently conceptualise young people and the ways in which they fit into our broader social, political and economic blueprint.

Critics (Patrick, 2013; Peters, 2003) have argued that we have firmly entered the age of 'knowledge capitalism', where intellectual and emotional labour (as opposed to physical) have attained significant importance in relation to economic growth and productivity. Fisher's quote at the beginning of this chapter encapsulates what many academics, teachers, young people, and parents increasingly 'feel': that education (like most social institutions) is under threat from the 'business ontology' of the neoliberal agenda. Patrick (2013, p. 2) has suggested that neoliberalism in contemporary educational policy has tended to reflect 'a technical rationalist approach to knowledge and its value'. That is, education has been incorporated into an agenda of economic productivity at the nation-state level and there has been an assumption that education will be a driver for economic growth, development and improved competitiveness for nations under globalised market conditions (Patrick, 2013). Accordingly, neoliberal reforms in education have nudged state provision towards privatisation and marketisation, and the language of 'new managerialism' has become increasingly prominent (Beckman *et al.*, 2009). Whitty (2000) has suggested that the belief is now firmly that the private sector approach is superior to that traditionally adopted in the public sector.

Accordingly, intellectual and symbolic 'goods' matter more than ever to the economy and the intellectual and affective resources of 'knowledge workers' have become highly significant market resources in and of themselves (Peters and Reveley, 2012; Tsogas, 2012). As the idea of the 'knowledge economy' takes hold, it follows that *individuals* carry the mode of production within them, and that 'shaping' their intellectual and affective resources must take place to ensure optimal development of human capital and economic growth. The value of education and knowledge production within such a system becomes tied to its ability to foster human capital. As Patrick (2013, p. 2) has suggested, the role of schools and universities can now legitimately be thought of as the creation of the knowledge worker.

Paulo Freire (2000, p. 60) argued that 'the oppressed, as objects, as "things," have no purposes except those their oppressors prescribe for them'. Critics have argued that this has been particularly reflected in neoliberal educational policy. Changes imposed in the name of 'efficiency' and 'excellence' have been responsible for the narrowing of educational experiences and increasing production of uncritical thinkers (Giroux, 2002) who simply reflect the primary needs of the market, where people are treated as 'knowledge workers' and prepared for 'jobs,' with little space left for other important features of education and personal development (Beckman et al., 2009). For example, Noddings (2003, p. 260) has argued:

> The best schools should resemble the best homes. What should we mean by *best*? The best homes provide continuity of caring relations, attend to and continuously evaluate both inferred and expressed needs, protect from harm without deliberately inflicting pain, communicate so as to develop common and individual interests, work together cooperatively, promote joy in genuine learning, guide moral and spiritual development (including the development of an uneasy conscience), contribute to the appreciation of the arts and other great cultural achievements, encourage love of place and protection of the natural world, and educate for both self-understanding and group understanding. The best homes and schools are happy places.

Brown (2015) recently critiqued a suite of authoritarian neoliberal policies in UK education that, she argues, have served to erode 'care' and 'relationship' in an education system that clearly values discipline and control above all else. Brown (2015) highlighted policy moves to 'ban best friends' and convert 'troops to teachers' as clear examples of the extent to which UK policy has sought to micro-manage children's educational lives to maximise control and production *at the expense*, she argues, of care and relationship. What is more, in neoliberal society care *itself* is now bought, sold and offered as a commodity (Hartford, 2010), and the nonmarket work of everyday care (in familial and extended contexts) has been explicitly excluded from most economic and political analyses of what matters (England and Folbre, 2006). There is a significant risk that such features of the educative process are increasingly marginalised in the neoliberal educational landscape.

On another note, Giroux (1988, p. 17) has suggested that education should

> support students' ability to act on and change personal conditions and social injustice. It should prepare young people to participate actively and critically in public life, support a sense of possibility, and arm young people with tools to survive and thrive in the face of multiple forms of oppression and marginalization.

Giroux (2002) argues that the neoliberal agenda has seduced academics, teachers and students into ignoring or devaluing issues such as social justice, care and empowerment, superseding democratic impulses and practices by completely overemphasising market-driven values. Ultimately, for many critics the 'business ontology' championed by the neoliberal agenda is simply incompatible with fostering and nurturing human potential and fulfilment, something (arguably) that ought to occupy a central position in the provision of education.

Sullivan (2002, p. 143) has suggested that the major risk associated with neoliberal ideology is that it has hijacked and perverted the very values that characterise social life:

> Private property has made us stupid and partial, that an object is only ours when we have it, when it exists for us as capital or when it is directly eaten, drunk, worn, inhabited, etc., in short utilized in some way [Marx 1966]. Instead, we realize our true human potential not through the possession of material objects, but through productive, creative activity, through the expression of our unique individuality by which we achieve recognition and spiritual satisfaction . . . the perversion of value is the symptom of a trend by which economic relations replace social relations, and the intrinsic value of goods is replaced by their external commodity value. Under capitalism, everything ceases to be valuable for itself or by virtue of its inner (e.g., artistic, ethical) value; a thing [perhaps even a person] has value only as a ware bought and sold on the market.

The changing nature of higher education

As knowledge capitalism has taken root in higher education, corporate values have gained increasing ascendency in a domain that was once regarded as a civil stronghold, where society could nurture and uphold democratic principles, helping academics and students alike become critical citizens with a sense of personal agency. Giroux (2002) has discussed the increasing emergence of a university culture where 'academic disciplines gain stature almost exclusively through their exchange value on the market' (p. 432), knowledge is viewed as a form of venture capital (creating an explosion of 'academic entrepreneurs') and bodies of research and ideas grounded in critical paradigms or incongruent with corporate values and aims are marginalised.

At the time of writing, there are emerging concerns in the UK about universities beginning to enforce academic redundancies based upon whether or not staff can satisfy economic performance metrics. For example, *Times Higher Education* (Grove, 2014) recently reported:

> Plans to make up to 50 academics redundant at the University of Warwick using 'simplistic' metrics have been criticised by staff. About 15 staff in Warwick's School of Life Sciences have been informed that their jobs are at risk after the department was told that it is failing to hit its financial targets. Another 30 positions at the Warwick Medical School are also believed to be at risk next year for the same reason . . . president of Warwick's University

and College Union branch said that a 'single cash metric' used to identify redundancies in life sciences had caused concern. Under the selection criteria, professors, associate professors and principal research fellows who did not have an average external grant income of at least £75,000 a year over the past four years are at risk.

It has been argued (Nussbaum, 2012; Patrick, 2013) that a university system that values knowledge in relation to its economic and practical utility has come to prioritise and elevate the status of the applied sciences, business and marketing and communication and information technology. This has often been at the expense of the arts and humanities, which, Nussbaum (2012, p. 23) argues, have been feared by those who view education as a tool for economic growth because '. . . it is easier to treat people as objects to manipulate if you have never learned any other way to see them'.

For many critics (Ball, 2012; Cribb and Gerwitz, 2013; Patrick, 2013), the last thirty years have witnessed the creation of a system of inequality in higher education in relation to how knowledge itself is treated and valued. Simply put, knowledge linked to economic growth, market values and enterprise has attained elevated status. The result has been what Cribb and Gerwitz (2013) have termed the 'hollowing out' of universities and knowledge. That is, neoliberalism seems to have 'taken away the joy of learning, the creativity of teaching, and the formation of strong public intellectuals' (Baltodano, 2012, p. 489), leaving a lack of any distinctive social responsibility and 'no ethical *raison d'etre*' (Cribb and Gerwitz, 2013). As Patrick (2013) has pointed out, educational institutions have simply become part of a social and cultural reality 'identified with an economic value system that shapes all reality in its own image' (Brancaleone and O'Brien, 2011, p. 502). Within this system, the very definition and value of knowledge has been transformed, together with its mode of production and the everyday practices through which it is brought into being.

Butler and Spoelstra (2014) interviewed twenty-five professors and critically examined how these senior academics (at professorial level in the UK, the United States, Europe and Australia) experienced 'producing knowledge' under the regime of excellence that has increasingly been imposed upon academics. Some quotes from the professors interviewed in their study are nice illustrations of the changing nature of knowledge production in higher education:

> There is one good thing about the RAE [UK Research Assessment Exercise]: it doesn't matter what the fuck you publish, only where you publish it. So if you look at . . . people who are in senior positions . . . 15 years ago, would those people have got those positions? Would their work have been judged on an ideological level and, because it wasn't ideologically connected with various institutional requirements, would they have not been promoted to senior levels as opposed to an RAE/REF situation? *(Professor 14)*

> On the one hand I play the game, as other people do. But on the other hand, it doesn't mean that I actually think the game is the right one . . . The REF is the part that I don't like, but it's an unavoidable part of where we are now. *(Professor 19)*

> It [a piece of research he had been persuaded to adapt in order to fit into a highly rated journal] gave me my four-by-four [four publications with a 'four star' rating] in the last RAE. From an instrumental position, it gave me my professorship. But as a scholarship piece, it's disgusting. Yeah, it was really, really awful. And it was one that I hoped would sink without trace, and it did luckily. *(Professor 4)*

As these quotes suggest, those producing knowledge are increasingly servants of the regime of excellence that has hijacked higher education. It is becoming clear that the knowledge academics produce is also at risk of being 'hollowed out', devoid of ideology and values that have either personal meaning or fall outside of the parameters of the language of excellence (Butler and Spoelstra, 2014; Cribb and Gerwitz, 2013; Giroux, 2002; Patrick, 2013).

Furthermore, students and their families increasingly view university education (and education per se) as a 'means to an end', the end being a competitive advantage in the job market and the idea that the more credentials individuals possess (in the shape of certificates and degrees), the more marketable they will be. Within this mentality, the university becomes little more than a technical training centre in which students are conceptualised as consumers in a system that values profit, control, efficiency and production above all else (Giroux, 2002). Ultimately, as Levidow (2002) has suggested, now implicit in contemporary university life is the idea that higher education institutions ought to:

> Raise their own productivity in order to survive. They must package knowledge, deliver flexible education through ICT, provide adequate training for 'knowledge workers', and produce more of them at lower unit cost. While this scenario portrays universities as guiding social change, there is evidence of a reverse tendency: that they are becoming subordinate to corporate-style managerialism and income-maximization. (Levidow, 2002, p. 3)

The changing nature of schooling

As Gordon and Whitty (1997) have noted, in recent decades, governments in many Western countries have sought to restructure and deregulate education, sculpting its provision into what might be termed a 'quasi-market' reflecting the idea that schooling is a business. Levacic (1995) has outlined that quasi-markets in the context of public services tend to involve an active attempt by the state to separate 'purchaser from provider' and, in accordance with the principles of markets, develop an element of 'user choice' and 'competition' between providers. It is important to note that such markets, particularly in the context of educational provision in Western countries (such as England, the United States and NZ), have *only* been realised through *significant* government intervention via the introduction of educational policy that has clearly prioritised factors such as school autonomy, diversity and choice, private sector involvement, privatisation and accountability mechanisms (Gordon and Whitty, 1997). As Harvey (2005, p. 2) has suggested, by the logic of neoliberal rationality 'if markets do not exist ... then they must be created, by state action if necessary'. This has clearly been the case and in recent decades schools have been subjected to increasingly neoliberal policies inflicted upon them by New Right governments in the English-speaking world, and supported by the IMF and the World Bank across other parts of the globe (Arnove, 1996).

In the UK, the 1992 White Paper for England and Wales (DfE, 1992) outlined five important themes for the development of schooling: greater autonomy for schools, greater accountability, quality, diversity and increasing parental choice. As Gordon and Whitty (1997) noted, there has been increasing rhetoric emphasising the importance for parents of 'choosing' schools that are most suited to their children's needs. Such rhetoric has been predicated on the notion that all families will benefit from increasing choice and diversity. However, the choice parents make is more typically based upon social or class-based parameters, as opposed to a choice of educational ideals and philosophies (Gordon, 1994; Gordon and Whitty, 1997; OECD, 1994).

As Gordon and Whitty (1997) have outlined, in England especially there has been a cultural tendency for schools to be judged as 'good' (and hence a more popular choice for parents and families) if they are academically selective and made up of predominantly socially advantaged families. Hence, families who are in a position to 'choose' are choosing schools that most closely resemble the traditional academic model of education (i.e. the template modelled by highly selective grammar schools). Interestingly, even new types of school tend to be judged by such standards. Whitty *et al.*'s (1993) study showed that many parents identified that they had chosen new models of school for their children because they were literally perceived as 'the next best thing to grammar schools or elite private schools'. It follows that as schools themselves determine the criteria for enrolment, schools in a position to do so often seek to identify their success with an emphasis on such traditional academic virtues. Such schools (a) tend to attract those students most likely to display such virtues and (b) can become 'self-perpetuating oligarchies' (Hirsch, 1995), selecting only those students who are a reflection of the characteristics of the school population. Additionally, others are precluded from genuinely choosing such schools, and a system reflecting a genuine 'choice' for all is inhibited.

For many critics, the rhetoric around the benefits of choice and diversity in schools has simply masked the fact that these policy movements have served to ensure that schools become increasingly myopic in their focus upon traditional academic values (which is what the 'customers' want). Blackmore (1995, p. 53) suggested that paradoxically, the market simply 'exacerbates differences between schools on the basis of class, race and ethnicity, but does not encourage diversity in image, clientele, organisation, curriculum or pedagogy'. In reality, a competitive edge for schools in the quasi-market 'is maintained by conforming to the dominant image of a good school as being well uniformed, well-disciplined and academically successful' (Blackmore, 1995, p. 48). Ultimately, the effect of the development of a quasi-market in England has simply been the narrowing of the scope of education (Gordon and Whitty, 1997).

Furthermore, the move towards quasi-market educational provision has resulted in the increasing emphasis on accountability, performativity and the language of managerialism. As Gordon and Whitty (1997) note, in England it was once the case that school inspectorates (typically themselves long-serving teachers with a close relationship to educational institutions) worked first and foremost to support schools and teachers 'in' their work, as opposed to evaluating the adequacy 'of' their work. However, under new systems, agents responsible for accountability have become deliberately separated from educational agencies themselves and the Office for Standards in Education (OFSTED) engages private contractors to undertake school inspections on behalf of the state. The emphasis of such systems of accountability is on specific, measurable outputs, to which schools, teachers and pupils are held accountable. Schools are required to measure up to certain end goals. The publication of 'league tables' of schools reflects this and further propagates the dominant cultural belief that traditional academic standards are 'what matters' in relation to educational provision. It is assumed by many that such standards accurately measure the performance of schools and whether they are effective institutions.

High stakes testing

In relation to this, high stakes testing has become a central part of the lives of millions of pupils, teachers and parents across most of the Western world and beyond, and has been the subject of extensive debate and criticism. It involves national, standardised achievement tests, the results of which are part of the 'culture of accountability' used to evaluate schools, pupils and teachers. Ryan and Weinstein (2009) have highlighted that high stakes testing reform strategies are being discussed and implemented worldwide, from South Korea to North America. In the United States, an American Educational Research Association position statement issued in July, 2000 forwarded the following description:

> Many states and school districts mandate testing programs to gather data about student achievement over time and to hold schools and students accountable. Certain uses of achievement test results are termed 'high stakes' if they carry serious consequences for students or educators. Schools may be judged according to the school-wide average scores for their students. High school-wide scores may bring public praise or financial rewards; low scores may bring public embarrassment or heavy sanctions. For individual students, high

scores may bring a special diploma attesting to exceptional academic accomplishment; low scores may result in students being held back in grade or denied a high school diploma.

In an accountability culture, high stakes tests are seen as a means of raising academic standards, holding educators and students accountable for meeting those standards, and boosting public confidence in schools (Heubert and Hauser, 1999). In England, high stakes testing has been used for over twenty years (it was formally introduced during the 1988 educational reforms) and since 1992 the results have been the focus of school performance league tables. Periodic national tests (known as SATs) at 7, 11 and 14 years were introduced throughout the school system in a coordinated scheme of examinations and associated 'pupil-tracking technologies' (Allen, 2012). The implementation of SATs in England deviated substantially from the original intentions of the Task Group on Assessment and Testing (TGAT) (which initially sought to combine teacher-led formative assessment with external demands for accountability [DES, 1988]) and teacher-led assessment was quickly abandoned to make way for an emphasis upon external, nationally comparable tests.

Similarly, in the United States there are now well established standards and standardised testing requirements. When President Bush signed into law the No Child Left Behind (NCLB) Act, it became mandatory for all US states to develop standardised tests and accountability systems (Hursh, 2005). Furthermore, in the United States, test results are scrutinised in relation to state requirements in order to determine whether schools are making 'adequate yearly academic progress' (AYP); failure to make AYP frequently results in significant sanctions and conferral of 'in need of improvement' status (Hursh, 2005). Where schools are in need of improvement, 'students must be given the option to transfer to another public school that has not been identified for improvement' (US Department of Education, 2002a, p. 6), with transportation costs covered by the failing school.

Advocates of high stakes testing base their arguments around some fundamental discourses: (1) a pressing need to increase educational and economic productivity in the face of a growing global market economy, (2) a need to reduce educational inequality, (3) a need to improve objectivity in educational assessment and (4) a need to hold schools and teachers accountable for the academic standards of their pupils (Hursh, 2005). For example, arguing that all students must succeed educationally in order that they, and the nation, can succeed economically, Carl Hayden (New York Chancellor of Education, 1996–2002) suggested:

> The requirement that every child be brought to a Regents level of performance is revolutionary. It is a powerful lever for educational equity. It is changing for the better the life prospects of millions of young people, particularly poor and minority children who in the past would have been relegated to a low standards path. Too often, these children emerged from school without the skills and knowledge needed for success in an increasingly complex economy. (Hayden, 2001, p. 1)

Advocates have also claimed that the increased objectification and standardisation inherent in high stakes testing is a superior form of assessment to teacher-led evaluation. For example, in the 'Parents' Guide to No Child Left Behind', it is implied that the objective data (from standardised testing) will improve upon teacher-led assessment, which has previously been accused of inadequately identifying teacher and student failures. Accordingly, NCLB 'provides teachers with independent information about each child's strengths and weaknesses. With this knowledge, teachers can craft lessons to make sure each student meets or exceeds the standards' (US Department of Education, 2002b, p. 9).

In response, there has been a strong voice of criticism in relation to the growth of high stakes testing. Corno (2000) metaphorically described its proliferation as a 'Trojan Horse', a horse that was 'welcomed into our school doors without knowing what harm was hidden inside' (Marchant, 2004, p. 6). As time goes by, what was inside is becoming clearer, and criticism of the high stakes testing movement has arisen from multiple angles from multiple academic disciplines.

For example, a large body of educational research (Hursh, 2007; Lipman and Hursh, 2007; McLaren and Jaramillo, 2007; Tabb, 2002) has viewed the proliferation of high stakes testing as a direct outgrowth of a rise in neoliberal, global capitalist policy, viewing educational policies such as NCLB as attempts to pull education into line with the agenda of an administration which positions education as an 'issue of "national security" and an instrument of "economic prosperity"' (p. 79). Children's educational achievement is viewed as a means to an end, a means by which global economic interests might be furthered by more closely monitoring educational attainment (Hursh, 2007).

Another major argument against high stakes testing has been that if judgements are to be made concerning the relative quality of teachers, schools, districts or states, it is critical that test results are valid reflections of teaching quality and of effective policies. That is, if differences in student achievement can be attributed to something *other* than the quality of education provision (e.g. poverty), then the validity of judgements attributing such differences to educational quality is clearly questionable (Marchant, 2004). For example, standardised test scores have been shown to correlate strongly with family income, and a school's performance is often more a reflection of its average family income than of the quality of the teaching it provides. In the United States, Hursh (2005) identified that 83 per cent of the failing schools in New York were located in five major poor urban areas (New York City, Syracuse, Rochester, Buffalo, Yonkers [NYSSBA, 2002]). He went on to suggest that, under the NCLB mandate, these schools were often unfairly judged, penalised and made scapegoats in relation to poor provision of education, when their achievement-related deficiencies were more likely rooted in social class and poverty as opposed to deficient teaching.

An additional criticism has been that there is a pervasive belief among teachers that high stakes tests are too frequent, the results are not useful to them, are misunderstood, create scaremongering in parents and the public, and are unfair to minorities and ESL students (Haladyna *et al.*, 1991; Heubert and Hauser, 1999; Paris and Urdan, 2000; Urdan and Paris, 2000). The myopic focus upon high stakes testing and standardisation frequently pressurises teachers to 'teach to the test', focusing intensely on the skills and knowledge that are required for successful test results and ignoring more complex, abstract aspects of various subjects (and in some cases ignoring certain subjects altogether) (Hursh, 2005). For example, Lipman's (2004) ethnographic investigation of schools in Chicago demonstrated how teachers' creativity and ingenuity in relation to literacy goals were frequently undermined by the pressure to teach to standardised tests. She documented a distinct conflict between teachers feeling able to help pupils develop knowledge and skills that might best equip them to understand *their* world and the development of knowledge and skills that would help them pass the standardised tests imposed upon them.

At pupil level, the practice of high stakes testing has been criticised on the grounds that it is dehumanising. Under pressure from above, schools are increasingly focused upon one thing – high test scores. For many educational researchers (Hursh, 2005; Reyes, 2007; Thomas, 2005), test scores have simply become a method by which pupils are reduced to a numerical value that 'discards what makes them human, unique, and vulnerable' (Reyes, 2007, p. 3) and renders 'the extraordinary, awe-inspiring diversities (developmental, cultural, personal, social) inherent in our children into a single indicator – a test score' (McNeil, 2005, p. 93). This makes schools ripened sites for social control, indoctrination and overt surveillance of children and young people (Allen, 2012; McNeil, 2005; McLaren and Jaramillo, 2007; Reyes, 2007).

Numerous researchers have therefore called for reconsideration, re-evaluation and reconstruction of an education system that places high stakes testing at its core (Thomas, 2005). Nichols and Berliner (2008, p. 676) have eloquently summarised the views of many contemporary academics on the topic of high stakes testing policies:

> High-stakes testing seems to help with preparing us for the vicissitudes of a competitive world economy, and so it is easily embraced. The needs of the emerging gerontocracy and those who already have some status in society are served by high-stakes testing . . . We oppose it for the same reason we are against forcing everyone to participate in extreme sports. If any person voluntarily chooses to jump the Grand Canyon on a motorcycle, scale Everest, or BASE jump, we wish them luck. We just don't think everyone should be required to engage in the same high stakes sports because, if everyone did, lots of people would be hurt . . . not all of us should be forced to take and fail such exams. In the current high-stakes environment, teachers, students, parents, and American education are being hurt by required high-stakes testing. This policy is corrupting our education system and needs to be stopped.

Accountability and performativity

As the above sections outline, it is hard to deny that teachers and academics alike are now working in a culture of increasing accountability. In relation to teachers, Gleeson and Gunter (2001) have documented this change in the UK, noting the considerable shift in the degree of autonomy that has been given to teachers. For example, they have described the period between the 1960s and mid-1980s as a period of 'relative autonomy'. In this period, teachers were more accountable to themselves (through informal reflection and peer review), worked within curricula established by head teachers and had their performance informally assessed with an emphasis on ethical commitment. The mid-1980s to 1990s have been described as a period of 'controlled autonomy'. During this period, senior management teams set up systems of formal surveillance and compulsory 'appraisals' were introduced in 1991. Furthermore, formal classroom observations and personal development targets were introduced as performance management mechanisms.

As Perryman (2006) has highlighted, from 1988 to 1994, a series of education acts were passed that led to teachers becoming a 'technical workforce to be managed and controlled' (p. 148) rather than a respected, autonomous profession. Since the 1988 Education Reform Act, accountability has shifted for teachers, from accountability to themselves, colleagues and students, to accountability to external agencies such as the Qualifications and Curriculum Authority (QCA), OfSTED and the Teacher Training Agency (TTA) (Perryman, 2006). Such a shift clearly reflected governmental and cultural discourse that the teaching profession was in need of reform, surveillance, monitoring and management. As Avis (2005, p. 211) has suggested, such accountability systems are now so pervasive that they might be viewed as a 'regime of truth that refuses other conceptualisations of good practice, which therefore become silenced and are denied legitimacy'.

From 2000, Gleeson and Gunter (2001) have suggested that teachers have been part of a system of 'productive autonomy'. That is, they have been held accountable through increasingly formal audits of student learning outcomes and test scores that are controlled by senior management. Teaching is controlled and dictated to teachers through the national curriculum and performance management systems such as performance-related pay and target setting. Surveillance and monitoring is undertaken based upon a scrutiny of an array of indicators, such as pupil outcomes, lesson observations and personal statements. As Perryman (2006, p. 149) has noted, 'pupils become objects and targets and the head teacher and senior management team are publicly accountable'.

What is more, by such standards of accountability, if a school in the UK is not thought to offer an acceptable standard of education, it is designated as 'Special Measures' and is subject to regular visits from Her Majesty's Inspectorate (HMI) to monitor progress. If the school is deemed to have sufficiently improved, it is removed from Special Measures following a full inspection. However, the school is closed down if OfSTED does not identify sufficient improvement (Perryman,

2006). As Perryman (2006) has noted, by September 1999, 900 schools (3 per cent of secondary schools) had been put into Special Measures in the UK.

Increasing accountability has led to an educational culture of 'performativity'. Lyotard (1984) first wrote about performativity in his critique of post-modern society's obsession with efficiency, effectiveness and judgement according to outcomes and performance. Ball (2003, p. 211) has defined performativity as follows:

> Performativity is a technology, a culture and a mode of regulation that employs judgements, comparisons and displays as means of incentive, control, attrition and change based on rewards and sanctions (both material and symbolic). The performances (of individual subjects or organizations) serve as measures of productivity or output, or displays of 'quality', or 'moments' of promotion or inspection. As such they stand for, encapsulate or represent the worth, quality or value of an individual or organization within a field of judgement.

Ball (2003) has highlighted the unpalatable changes in the life world of teachers, caught up in a performative education system. For example, he has written of the 'values schizophrenia' created when practitioners are required to organise themselves and their professional lives so that they are able to satisfy targets, indicators and evaluations based around the production of standards in the children they initially signed up to educate. Under this regime of governance, teachers are increasingly required to set aside personal values and commitment to education in order to fabricate a veneer of professional competence for which they are held accountable. Inside, for many, a sense of deep internal conflict, dissatisfaction, inauthenticity and a dampened sense of personal agency increasingly characterise their professional life (Ball, 2003). Jeffrey and Woods (1998), in their book *Testing Teachers*, provide evidence of how such performative cultures invade and colonise teachers' lives, rob them of their autonomy and de-professionalise them. As one teacher quoted in the book suggests:

> I don't have the job satisfaction now I once had working with young kids because I feel every time I do something intuitive I just feel guilty about it. Is this right; am I doing this the right way; does this cover what I am supposed to be covering: should I be doing something else: should I be more structured; should I have this in place; should I have done this? You start to query everything you are doing and there's a kind of guilt in teaching at the moment. I don't know if that's particularly related to Ofsted but of course it's multiplied by the fact that Ofsted is coming in because you get in a panic that you won't be able to justify yourself when they finally arrive. (p. 118)

A quote from a senior secondary school manager in Perryman's (2006) study also nicely captures the 'theatrical displays' performed by teachers under increasing pressure to 'reproduce excellence' for school inspection agencies:

We got very, very good at applying the very bland OfSTED model to our teaching. Why don't you get OfSTED to come and analyse theatre plays and concerts because they know the exact formula that makes them successful and satisfactory? We got very good at producing OfSTED satisfactory type lessons and this is all very well but teaching is an art as well as a science, and if you take all the artistry out of it where is it going to go? (p. 155)

What is concerning is the way in which performative cultures have served to construct new subjectivities (Ball, 2003). That is, they shape and sculpt new ways of being, 'persuading' and 'seducing' teachers, students and academics towards particular sorts of educational 'selves' that have far reaching impacts on internal life.

The commodified learner

Ultimately, the invasion of education by the language of new performance management has served to redefine what it *means* to be a learner (and, for that matter, a teacher and/or academic). In *The Birth of Biopolitics*, Foucault suggested that it is a fallacy to assume that market principles, such as competition, individualism and performance according to externally imposed standards are a part of the *natural* order of things. Rather, such ideals, values and principles 'must be actively instituted, maintained, reassessed and, if need be, reinserted at all levels of society' (Foucault, 2008, p. 20). Hence, for Foucault, the good and virtuous person in neoliberal society, *Homo economicus*, must be fostered through social and institutional mechanisms that are persuasively and seductively ordered and organised around these market values (Hamann, 2009). Forms of subjectivity must be constructed, brought into being and maintained by social mechanisms of subjectification. As Hamann (2009) has suggested, 'economic man' is therefore a subject that must be 'produced'. In essence, social and cultural mechanisms and practices create the conditions designed to shape individual conduct (Dreyfus and Rabinow, 1983; Foucault, 1996) and, in neoliberal society, performative cultures and the language of new performance management have been a significant 'technology'.

In order to 'produce' economic man, the values and principles of neoliberalism must be increasingly positioned at the core of an existence where market-based identities (e.g. individualism, performativity, competition, economic gain, productivity) predominate (Carr and Batlle, 2015). To this end, as this chapter has highlighted, there has been a steady normalisation of increasingly controlling and invasive institutional practices (e.g. systems of accountability, performativity, efficiency, transparency) that have sought to legitimise and firmly situate such values at the heart of all educational life (Ball, 2003). Neoliberalism is quite literally 'reformulating personhood, psychological life, moral and ethical responsibility, and what it means to have selfhood and identity' (Sugarman, 2015, p. 105). Martin and McLellan (2013) have made a convincing case for the idea that the ideal 'commodified learner' in neoliberal society can now be conceptualised as a rational and strategic self-manager, able to monitor, strategise, reinforce and motivate themselves in pursuit of notions of what it means to be 'excellent,' 'high quality' or 'professional,' constructs that have been hijacked and redefined by the language of new public management.

Neoliberalism: flawed logic?

There has been an inevitable concern that the concept of neoliberalism has become bloated, so bloated that it seems difficult to see how it could coherently capture the diverse array of projects, initiatives and institutions that have been labelled as 'neoliberal' (Heynen et al., 2007). Such diversity, some might argue, renders the term neoliberalism inadequate to convey the temporal and spatial evolution and adaptation of governance projects and policy that, while perhaps *inspired* by neoliberal logic, are transformed into something distinct in the messiness of politics and lived experiences. Indeed, for Barnett (2005), the term may even have become a convenient 'go to' for left-leaning academics and ultimately may blind them to the pluralities inherent in the diverse array of policies and political struggles across social contexts. In this book, however, I share Heynen et al.'s (2007) view that neoliberalism is, nonetheless, an abstraction well worth identifying, exploring and critiquing:

> How to capture important continuities and connections in diverse transformations going on around the world over a period of many years is no simple task, and any effort to do so requires observers to engage in some degree of abstraction. And yet something is going on worth naming. We insist on the analytical and political purchase of identifying, albeit reflexively, the pervasive 'metalogics' of what we see around us, not least because we see a fairly common set of discourses, ideologies and practices that remain the most dominant development in social regulation in the post-Keynesian era. (Heynen et al., 2007, p. 4)

As Bourdieu (1998) has noted (in relation to the 'metalogics' of neoliberalism), it is a complete fiction that market principles are self-regulating and can operate above or outside the realms of society. For Bourdieu (1998), neoliberalism has simply been a utopian project that has sought to pursue narrow aims, imposing upon societies the economic and social conditions and structures necessary for its realisation. However, in domains such as education it has become obvious that the pursuit of this utopian ideal cannot take place without attempting to modify human beings in accordance with market values. The problem, as Robertson (2007) has noted, is simple: human beings will resist these pressures because people, labour, land, knowledge, education and health are *not meant* to be conceptualised as commodities. Furthermore, as Polanyi (1944) suggested some time ago, it is *unethical* to treat as, and sculpt, nature and human beings into commodities. It is also *unethical* for governments to attempt to 'insert' these market values into people's lives.

Robertson (2007) has suggested that on the one hand, it has become clear that in the midst of market economies, governments have been faced with a quandary. That is, if the state is 'creating' the social and economic conditions upon which market values thrive, who is looking after citizens? On the other hand, if the state sees its role as protecting and supporting its citizens, doesn't this sometimes mean imposing restrictions on the market? Too few restrictions, however, and the state risks prioritising capital over citizens (Robertson, 2007), threatening both democracy and social justice. In essence, the main problem with the movement toward markets that characterises neoliberal society is that it requires an alternative movement to keep it in check (e.g. the state, civil society). However, rebalancing things in favour of the state also illuminates the basic contradictions inherent in neoliberalism: it is simply an unviable political project given its propensity to generate social instability, social polarisation and social injustice (Brodie, 2007; Robertson, 2007).

There is ample evidence that neoliberalism in its global form has failed to deliver greater equality and reduced poverty across the world. It has been well documented (ILO, 2004; UN, 2005; UNDP, 2005) that economic globalisation has resulted in slowed economic growth, enormous increases in inequality and poverty, and isolation of the 'fourth world' of Sub-Saharan Africa (Robertson, 2007, p. 13). In relation to education, neoliberalism has ultimately brought about a decline in expenditure on education across the globe (apart from in Latin America). Interestingly, however, the decline has not been 'felt' by those who have been most able to benefit from neoliberal social and economic policies (Robertson, 2007). As has been discussed above, market values have transformed education into a sector where those with social and economic capital are able to secure for themselves 'higher quality' education, reinforcing class distinctions (e.g. Giroux, 2002; Gordon and Whitty, 1997). Meanwhile, those from poorer neighbourhoods have been forced into under-chosen schools, which are blamed, penalised and chastised for underperformance (Hursh, 2005). Quality has become synonymous with a narrow set of indicators and league tables, the access to which is invariably more available to those with the most significant resources (Ball, 2003).

Moreover, as Lorenz (2012) has noted, while the transformation of education across sectors has been radical, the colonisation of schools and universities by the language of managerialism has never seriously been up for discussion. This, he argues, is a reflection of the hegemony of neoliberalism. Absurdly, as Lorenz (2012) has argued, there is really no convincing evidence at all that the radical educational shift under neoliberalism has been beneficial. Conversely, there is a wealth of evidence that transforming education into a production line that (a) values only those ideas its managers believe will sell, (b) treats employees and learners as though they were too devious or stupid to be trusted and (c) values managerial process above all else simply doesn't work for educating *people* (Lorenz, 2012).

In relation to higher education, Lorenz (2012) has suggested that there are three types of statements playing a key role in the neoliberal discourse that has hijacked education: (1) assumptions that view the quality of education as synonymous with some measure of quantity of educational output, (2) statements that identify the academic worth of research (and researchers) as synonymous with their economic value and (3) statements that seek to evaluate the value of (typically) underfunded universities by the same yardstick as elite institutions. For Lorenz (2012), such assumptions are, quite simply, bullshit. In his essay 'On Bullshit', Frankfurt (2005) outlines how bullshit is not particularly based on a belief that what is being claimed is true – nor (as with a lie) that it is untrue – 'it is just this lack of connection to a concern with truth – this indifference to how things really are – that is the essence of bullshit' (pp. 33–4). As Lorenz (2012, p. 627) has noted:

> This specific characteristic of bullshit can explain why many faculty members seem so remarkably helpless when up against the NPM [new public management] bullshit of management. Those who sell NPM bullshit neither observe the rules of science nor break them; the NPM bullshitter is simply playing a completely different game from that played by the faculty. This is a game that neoliberal policy has superimposed over scholarship in the universities in the form of a management tier – with substantial help from within the university walls, of course. The bullshitter, in sum, is only interested in effects and does not necessarily believe in what he states himself.

As a consequence of such bullshit, the morale and spirit of teachers and academics is under threat, and academic knowledge is literally being 'hollowed out,' as researchers become knowledge entrepreneurs. Brodie (2007, p. 105) has eloquently captured the current state of affairs:

> The ultimate paradox of our neoliberal times is that the historically unprecedented human capacity to enhance and secure human wellbeing, locally and globally, should generate such degrees of precarious existence for the vast majority of humanity, indeed for all things living . . . In the face of all of this, the necessary task of reforming social justice may very well hinge upon our collective insistence on putting the social back into our way of seeing and contesting neoliberal times. Contemporary politics invite us to seriously reflect upon a time-worn adage: if you wish peace, care for justice.

In this book, I echo Brodie's sentiments. Reconstructing or reclaiming education in neoliberal society is a complex challenge that, to a large extent, depends upon the mobilisation of a collective critical consciousness. Taylor (2003) has argued that it is time for academics to 'step up to the plate', recognising that they have so far been predominantly morally myopic and/or complicit in the hijacking of educational provision. In what follows, I explore the possibility that educational psychologists might think more critically and politically in relation to the ways in which they contribute to such efforts.

References

Allen, A. (2012). Cultivating the myopic learner: The shared project of high-stakes and low-stakes assessment. *British Journal of Sociology of Education*, 33(5), 641–59.
Arnove, R. (1996). Neo-Liberal Education Policies in Latin America: Arguments in Favor and Against. Paper delivered to the Comparative and International Education Society, Williamsburg, March 6–10.
Avis, J. (2005). Beyond performativity: Reflections on activist professionalism and the labour process in further education. *Journal of Education Policy*, 20(2), 209–22.
Ball, S.J. (2003). The teacher's soul and the terrors of performativity. *Journal of Educational Policy*, 18, 215–28.
Ball, S.J. (2012). Show Me the Money! Neoliberalism at work in education. *FORUM: For Promoting 3–19 Comprehensive Education*, 54(1), 23–8.
Baltodano, M. (2012). Neoliberalism and the demise of public education: The corporatization of schools of education. *International Journal of Qualitative Studies in Education*, 25(4), 487–507.
Barnett, C. (2005). The Consolations of Neoliberalism. *Geoforum*, 36(1), 7–12.
Barnett, C. (2010). Publics and markets: What's wrong with neoliberalism? In S.J. Smith, R.Pain, S.A. Marston and J.P. Jones III (eds), *The Sage Handbook of Social Geography* (pp. 269–96). London: Sage.
Beckman, A., Cooper, C. and Hill, D. (2009). Neoliberalization and managerialization of 'education' in England and Wales – a case for reconstructing education. *Journal for Critical Education Policy Studies*, 7(2), 311–45.
Black, P. and Wiliam, D. (1998). *Inside the Black Box: Raising Standards Through Classroom Assessment*. London: King's College London School of Education.
Blackmore, J. (1995). Breaking out from a masculinist politics of education. In B. Limerick and B. Lingard (eds), *Gender and Changing Educational Management* (pp. 44–56). Rydalmere, NSW: Hodder Education.
Boas, T.C. and Gans-Morse, J. (2009). Neoliberalism: From new liberal philosophy to anti-liberal slogan. *Studies in Comparative International Development*, 44(2), 137–61.
Bourdieu, P. (December 1998) Utopia of Endless Exploitation: The essence of neoliberalism, *Le Monde Diplomatique*. Available at http://mondediplo.com/1998/12/08bourdieu.
Brancaleone, D. and O'Brien, S. (2011). Educational commodification and the (economic) sign value of learning outcomes. *British Journal of Sociology of Education*, 32(4), 501–19.
Briggs, A. (1961). The welfare state in historical perspective. *European Journal of Sociology*, 2(2), 221–58.
Brodie, J. (2007). Reforming social justice in neoliberal times. *Studies in Social Justice*, 1(2), 93–107.
Brown, C. (2015). *Educational Binds of Poverty: The Lives of School Children*. Abingdon, Oxon: Routledge.
Brown, W. (2003). Neo-liberalism and the End of Liberal Democracy. *Theory and Event*, 7(1), 1–43.
Butler, N. and Spoelstra, S. (2014). The Regime of Excellence and the Erosion of Ethos in Critical Management Studies. *British Journal of Managemement*, 25(3), 538–50.
Carr, S. and Batlle, I.C. (2015). Attachment theory, neoliberalism, and social Conscience. *Journal of Theoretical and Philosophical Psychology*, 35(3), 160–76.
Coakley, J. (2011). Ideology doesn't just happen: Sports and neoliberalism. *Curitiba*, 1(1), 67–84.
Corno, L. (2000). Comments on trojan horse papers. *Issues in Education*, 6, 125–31.

Cribb, A. and Gewirtz, S. (2013). The hollowed-out university? A critical analysis of changing institutional and academic norms in UK higher education. *Discourse*, *34*(3), 338–50.

DfE [Department for Education]. (1992). *Choice and Diversity*. London: Her Majesty's Stationery Office.

Dreyfus, H. and Rabinow, P. (1983). *Michel Foucault: Beyond Structuralism and Hermeneutics*. Chicago: University of Chicago Press.

England, P. and Folbre, N. (2006). Capitalism and the erosion of care. In A. Wharton (ed.), *Working in America: Continuity, Conflict, and Change* (pp. 495–510). New York: McGraw Hill.

Fisher, M. (2009). *Capitalist Realism: Is There No Alternative?* Ropley, Hants: Zero Books.

Foucault, M. (1996). *Istoria nebuniei în perioada clasică*. Bucuresti: Humanitas.

Foucault, M. (2008). *The Birth of Biopolitics: Lectures at the Collège de France, 1978–1979*, translated by G. Burchell. In A.I. Davidson (ed.), New York: Palgrave Macmillan.

Frankfurt, H.G. (2005). *On Bullshit*. Princeton: Princeton University Press.

Freire, P. (1974). *Education for Critical Consciousness*. London: Sheed and Ward.

Giroux, H.A. (1988). *Schooling and the Struggle for Public Life*. Minneapolis, MN: University of Minnesota Press.

Giroux, H.A. (2002). Neoliberalism, corporate culture, and the promise of higher education: The university as a democratic public sphere. *Harvard Educational Review*, *72*(4), 425–63.

Giroux, H.A. (2003). Zero tolerance, domestic militarization, and the war against youth. *Social Justice*, *30*(2), 59–65.

Giroux, H.A. (2005). The terror of neoliberalism: Rethinking the significance of cultural politics. *College Literature*, *32*(1), 1–19.

Gleeson, D. and Gunter, H. (2001). The performing school and the modernisation of teachers. In D. Gleeson and C. Husbands (eds), *The Performing School*. London: Routledge, Falmer.

Gordon, L. (1994). 'Rich' and 'Poor' schools in Aotearoa, New Zealand. *New Zealand Journal of Educational Studies*, 29(2), 113–125.

Gordon, L. and Whitty, G. (1997). Giving the 'hidden hand' a helping hand? The rhetoric and reality of neoliberal education reform in England and New Zealand. *Comparative Education*, *33*(3), 453–67.

Grove, J. (2014). Simplistic redundancy metrics criticized. *Times Higher Education Supplement*, 16 October 2014. Available at www.timeshighereducation.co.uk/news/simplistic-redundancy-metrics-criticised/2016357.article.

Haladyna, T., Nolen, S.B. and Haas, N.S. (1991). Raising standardized achievement scores and the origins of test score pollution. *Educational Researcher*, *20*(5), 2–7.

Hamann, T. (2009). Neoliberalism, governmentality, and ethics. *Foucault Studies*, *6*, 37–59.

Hartford, I. (2010). My work utopia: pursuing a satisfactory work life amid an alienating world. *Human Architecture: Journal of the Sociology of Self-Knowledge*, *8*, 167–76.

Harvey, D. (2005). *A Brief History of Neoliberalism*. Oxford: Oxford University Press.

Harvey, D. (2007). Neoliberalism as creative destruction. *The ANNALS of the American Academy of Political and Social Science*, *610*(1), 21–44.

Hayden, C. (7 May 2001). *Letter to the Hon. Richard Brodsky and Hon. Richard Green*. New York: State Assembly.

Hayek, F.A. (1979). *Law, Legislation and Liberty: A New Statement of the Liberal Principles and Political Economy. Volume III: The Political Order of a Free People*. London: Routledge.

Heubert, P. and Hauser, R.M. (1999). *High Stakes: Testing for Tracking, Promotion and Graduation*. Washington, DC: National Academy of Sciences.

Heynen, N., McCarthy, J., Prudham, S. and Robbins, P. (2007). Introduction: False promises. In N. Heynen, J. McCarthy, S. Prudham and P. Robbins (eds), *Neoliberal Environments: False Promises and Unnatural Consequences* (pp. 1–22). London: Routledge.

Hirsch, D. (1995). The other school choice: How oversubscribed schools select their students. Paper presented in a public lecture at London Institute of Education, London, May.

Hursh, D. (2005). The growth of high-stakes testing in the USA: Accountability, markets and the decline in educational equality. *British Educational Research Journal*, *31*(5), 605–22.

Hursh, D. (2007). 'Assessing No Child Left Behind' and the rise of neoliberal education policies. *American Educational Research Journal*, *44*(3), 493–518.

ILO. (2004). *A Fair Globalization: Creating Opportunities for All, the World Commission on the Social Dimensions of Globalization*. Geneva: ILO.

Jeffrey, B. and Woods, P. (1998). *Testing Teachers: The Effect of School Inspections on Primary Teachers*. East Sussex BN3 2FA, UK: Psychology Press.

Kendall, G. (2003). What is neoliberalism? In *TASA Conference* (pp. 1–6). Australia: University of New England.

Larner, W. (2000). Neo-liberalism: Policy, ideology, governmentality. *Studies in Political Economy*, *63*, 5–25.

Larner, W. (2006). Review of a brief history of neoliberalism. *Economic Geography*, *82*(4), 449–51.

Levacic, R. (1995). *Local Management of Schools: Analysis and Practice*. Milton Keynes, Bucks: Open University Press.

Levidow, L. (2002). Marketizing higher education: Neoliberal strategies and counter-strategies. In K. Robins and F. Webster (eds), *The Virtual University? Knowledge, Markets and Management* (pp. 227–48). Oxford, UK: Oxford University Press.

Lipman, P. (2004). *High-Stakes Education: Inequality, Globalization and Urban School Reform*. New York: Routledge.

Lipman, P. and Hursh, D. (2007). Renaissance 2010: The reassertion of ruling-class power through neoliberal policies in Chicago. *Policy Futures in Education*, *5*(2), 160–78.

Locke, J. (1689). *Two Treatises of Government*. London: Awnsham Churchill.

Lorenz, C. (2012). If you're so smart, why are you under surveillance? Universities, neoliberalism, and new public management. *Critical Inquiry*, *38*(3), 599–629.

Lyotard, J.F. (1984). *The Postmodern Condition: A Report on Knowledge* (Vol. 10). Manchester: Manchester University Press.

Marchant, G.J. (2005). What is at stake with high stakes testing? A discussion of issues and research, *Ohio Journal of Science*, *104*(2), 2–7.

Martin, J. and McLellan, A. (2013). *The Education of Selves: How Psychology Transformed Students*. New York, NY: Oxford University Press.

McLaren, P. and Jaramillo, N. (2007). *Pedagogy and Praxis in the Age of Empire: Toward a new Humanism*. Netherlands: Sense Publishers.

McNeil, L.M. (2005). Faking equity: High stakes testing and the education of Latino youth. In A. Valenzuela (ed.), *Leaving Children Behind: How 'Texas Style' Accountability Fails Latino Youth* (pp. 57–111). Albany, NY: State University of New York Press.

New York State School Boards Association. (2002). *Title i accountability status updated for March, 2003*. Available at www.nyssba.org/adnews/misc/thenewaccountability-5.htm.

Nichols, S.L. and Berliner, D.C. (2008). Why has high-stakes testing so easily slipped into contemporary American life? *Phi Delta Kapan*, *89*(9), 672–76.

Noddings, N. (2003). *Happiness and Education*. Cambridge: Cambridge University Press.

Nozick, R. (1974). *Anarchy, State and Utopia*. Oxford: Blackwell.

OECD. (1994). *School: A Matter of Choice*. Paris: OECD.

Paris, S.G. and Urdan, T. (2000). Policies and practices of high-stakes testing that influence teachers and schools. *Issues in Education*, 6, 83–107.

Patrick, F. (2013). Neoliberalism, the knowledge economy, and the learner: Challenging the inevitability of the commodified self as an outcome of education. *International Scholarly Research Network: Education*, 2013, 1–8.

Perryman, J. (2006). Panoptic performativity and school inspection regimes: Disciplinary mechanisms and life under special measures. *Journal of Education Policy*, 21(2), 147–61.

Peters, M.A. (2003). Classical political economy and the role of universities in the new knowledge economy. *Globalisation, Societies and Education*, 1(2), 153–68.

Peters, M.A. and Reveley, J. (2014). Retrofitting drucker: Knowledge work under cognitive capitalism. *Culture and Organization*, 20(2), 135–51.

Polanyi, K. (1944). *The Great Transformation: The Political and Economic Origins of Our Time*. Boston: Beacon Press.

Read, J. (2009). A genealogy of homo-economicus: Neoliberalism as the production of subjectivity. *Foucault Studies*, 6, 25–36.

Robertson, S. (2007). 'Remaking the World': Neo-liberalism and the transformation of education and teachers' labour. In L. Weis and M. Compton (eds), *The Global Assault on Teachers, Teaching and Their Unions*. New York: Palgrave.

Ryan, R.M. and Weinstein, N. (2009). A self-determination theory perspective on high-stakes testing. *Theory and Research in Education*, 7(2), 224–33.

Smith, A. (1776). *An Inquiry Into the Nature and Causes of the Wealth of Nations*. In E. Cannan (ed.), London: Methuen. Available at www.econlib.org/library/Smith/smWNCover.html.

Sugarman, J. (2015). Neoliberalism and psychological ethics. *Journal of Theoretical and Philosophical Psychology*, 35(2), 103–16.

Sullivan, S. (2002). *Marx for a Post-Communist Era: On Poverty, Corruption, and Banality*. London and New York: Routledge.

Tabb, W. (2002). *Unequal Partners: A Primer on Globalization*. New York: The New Press.

Taylor, P. (2003). Humbolt's rift: Managerialism in education and complicit intellectuals. *European Political Science*, 3(1), 75–84.

Thatcher, M. (1987). 'Aids, education and the year 2000'. *Women's Own*, pp. 8–10.

Thomas, C. (2005). Paulo freire, Today's public schools and the pedagogy of the oppressed. *Journal of Philosophy and History of Education*, 55, 217–19.

Thorsen, D.E. (2010). The neoliberal challenge. What is Neoliberalism? *Contemporary Readings in Law and Social Justice*, 2(2), 188–214.

Thorsen, D.E. and Lie, A. (2006). *What is neoliberalism?* (Manuscript). Oslo: University of Oslo, Department of Political Science.

Tsogas, G. (2012). The commodity form in cognitive capitalism. *Culture and Organization*, 18(5), 377–95.

UN. (2005). The inequality predicament: Report on the world social situation 2005. *UN Department of Economic and Social Affairs*. Available at www.un.org/esa/socdev/rwss/rwss.htm.

UNDP. (2005). *Human Development Report 2005: International Cooperation at a Crossroads: Aid Trade and Security in an Unequal World*. New York: UNDP. Available at http://hdr.undp.org/reports/global/2005.

Urdan, T.C. and Paris, S.G. (1994). Teachers' perceptions of standardized achievement tests. *Educational Policy*, 8(2), 137–56.

US Department of Education, Office of Elementary and Secondary Education. (2002a). *No Child Left Behind: A Desk Reference*. Washington, DC: US Department of Education.

US Department of Education, Office of the Secretary. (2002b). *What to Know and Where to Go: A Parent's Guide to No Child Left Behind*. Washington, DC: US Department of Education.

Valenzuela, A. (1999). Subtractive schooling: US-Mexican youth and the politics of caring. Albany: State University of New York Press.

Weeden, P., Winter, J. and Broadfoot, P. (2002). *Assessment: What's in it for schools?* Abingdon: Routledge Falmer.

Whitty, G. (12 November 2000). Privatisation and Marketisation in education policy. Speech given to the National Union of Teachers conference Involving the Private Sector in Education: Value Added or High Risk? London. Available at http://k1.ioe.ac.uk/directorate/NUTPres%20web%20version%20(2%2001).

Whitty, G., Edwards, T. and Gewirtz, S. (1994). *Specialisation and Choice in Urban Education*. London: Routledge.

Wiliam, D. (1992). Value-added attacks: Technical issues in reporting national curriculum assessments. *British Educational Research Journal*, *18*(4), 329–41.

Wiliam, D. and Black, P. (1996). Meanings and consequences: A basis for distinguishing formative and summative functions of assessment? *British Educational Research Journal*, *22*(5), 537–48.

2
CREATING A CRITICAL SPACE

> With even the slightest reflection, it is easy to see that the discipline of psychology desperately needs the kind of reflective dialogue that we [theoretical and critical psychologists] are uniquely positioned to foster. This need is obvious in the societies in which we live. We need to understand that we have a great deal to offer and to act accordingly.
>
> (Fowers, 2015, p. 14)

In neoliberal society, the field of psychology is in need of a critical conscience. Sugarman (2015, p. 103) recently asked the following significant question: 'What is an ethics of psychology when interpreted in the context of a neoliberal political order'? He argued: (a) psychologists cannot understand and consider the ethical connotations of their disciplinary and professional practices if they are not ideologically aware and (b) when we open our eyes, comprehending the ideological reality of our neoliberal times, it is clear that psychology has taken little responsibility for genuinely challenging, critiquing and protecting people's welfare in the struggle against injustice. For Sugarman (2015, p. 103), such a lack of responsibility quite literally contravenes (1) Principle B of the American Psychological Association's *Ethical Principles of Psychologists and Code of Conduct* (American Psychological Association, 2010); (2) Principle IV of the *Canadian Code of Ethics for Psychologists* (Canadian Psychological Association, 2008) and (3) Principle 3 of the British Psychological Society's *Code of Ethics and Conduct* (British Psychological Society, 2009), all of which are concerned with psychologists' responsibility to society.

It has been suggested that neoliberalism is 'reformulating personhood, psychological life, moral and ethical responsibility, and what it means to have selfhood and identity' (Sugarman, 2015, p. 105). In *The Birth of Biopolitics*, Foucault (2008) suggested that it is a pure fallacy to suggest that market principles, such as competition, individualism, performativity and accountability are a part of the *natural* order of things. Rather, these ideals, values and principles 'must be actively instituted, maintained, reassessed and, if need be, reinserted at all levels of society' (Foucault, 2008, p. 20). Hence, for Foucault, the good and virtuous person in neoliberal society, *Homo Economicus* (Hamann, 2009), can only be fostered through social and institutional mechanisms that are persuasively and seductively ordered and organised around market values. Forms of subjectivity must be constructed, brought into being and maintained by social mechanisms of subjectification. As Hamann (2009) has suggested, 'economic man' is therefore a subject that must be 'produced'.

Foucault outlined the connection between neoliberal government and the construction of new subjectivities or ways of being. He used the term 'governmentality' to refer to the various and complex ways in which social, political and cultural institutions 'conduct the conduct' of individuals. In neoliberal society, Foucault (2008) saw features such as 'enterprise' and 'competition' as technologies of governance that have pervaded social institutions in neoliberal society, infiltrating human experience and the lifeworld of individuals. For example, writing about organisational cultures in his essay, 'The Essence of Neoliberalism', Bourdieu (1998) outlines how key neoliberal values (such as competition) have been woven into the structural fabric of organisational life, making them inescapable for many individuals:

> Competition is extended to individuals themselves, through the individualization of the wage relationship: establishment of individual performance objectives, individual performance evaluations, permanent evaluation, individual salary increases or granting of bonuses as a function of competence and of individual merit; individualized career paths; strategies of 'delegating responsibility' tending to ensure the self-exploitation of staff who, simple wage laborers in relations of strong hierarchical dependence, are at the same time held responsible for their sales, their products, their branch, their store, etc. as though they were independent contractors. This pressure toward 'self-control' extends workers' 'involvement' according to the techniques of 'participative management' considerably beyond management level. All of these are techniques of rational domination that impose over-involvement in work (and not only among management) and work under emergency or high-stress conditions. And they converge to weaken or abolish collective standards or solidarities. (para 8)

Sugarman (2015) has noted that such values and features of neoliberal society do not only pertain to institutional organisations. Rather, people themselves can be sculpted into enterprising, competitive creatures whose personalities, character and personal attributes align with the dominant culture. Accordingly, the economic well-being of the state is likely to be maximised in a society populated by *Homo Economicus*. Sugarman (2015, p. 104) has described *Homo Economicus* as follows:

They conceive of themselves as a set of assets – skills and attributes – to be managed, maintained, developed, and treated as ventures in which to invest. As enterprising subjects, we think of ourselves as individuals who establish and add value to ourselves through personal investment (in education or insurance), who administer ourselves as an economic interest with vocabularies of management and performativity (satisfaction, worth, productivity, initiative, effectiveness, skills, goals, risk, networking, and so forth), who invest in our aspirations by adopting expert advice (of psychotherapists, personal trainers, dieticians, life coaches, financial planners, genetic counselors), and who maximize and express our autonomy through choice (mostly in consumerism).

What is more, people do not simply surrender their identities to neoliberal aims and values without subtle (yet persuasive) forms of discourse and programs of rationality that prompt them to do so. Social and cultural spheres (such as medicine, science and education) that legitimise and reproduce neoliberal values and goals must also be brought into question (Binkley, 2011; Carr and Batlle, 2015; Gorz, 1999; Rose, 1999; Sugarman, 2015). In psychology, what has concerned some critics (Binkley, 2011; Carr and Batlle, 2015; Sugarman, 2015) has been the increasing tendency to incorporate *psychological* features of individuals' identities (e.g. discourses around 'self-control,' 'mental toughness', 'features of personality' or 'motivation') into the process of normalising neoliberal values. Increasingly, our psychological characteristics (our cognitive, emotional and relational selves) are deployed as the errand boy of super-ordinate aims and value structures that mirror market-based identities (Binkley, 2011). This edges closer to a hijacking of the worker's personality and raises uncomfortable ideas about psychology in relation to C. Wright Mills's (1959) famous concerns about persons becoming 'compliant robots' fitted to a society relentlessly pursuing capitalist ideology (Binkley, 2011).

As an intellectual domain dedicated to the generation of knowledge about the cognitive, emotional and social dimensions of human existence, critics have been concerned that psychology itself has been swept up in a tide that reflects and serves a neoliberal agenda in a myriad of ways (Binkley, 2011; Carr and Batlle, 2015; Rose, 1999; Sugarman, 2015). As an example, some authors (Binkley, 2011; Gore, 2010; Wilson, 2008) have reacted strongly to the emergence of the positive psychology movement which, they suggest, attempts to redefine the nature of psychological well-being so that it aligns individual and collective life with neoliberal values (see Binkley, 2011, for a thorough discussion). As Binkley (2011, p. 374) describes:

> At the centre of these efforts is the belief that happiness results from the cognitive outlook of individuals: to the extent that people can be brought to assess their situations and themselves in a favourable light, the resulting emotional flush will move them to perform . . . on a superior level . . . The new discourse on happiness has influenced a range of institutional, managerial,

and planning activities, variously centred on the government of individuals, communities, and organisations, through appeals to their capacity to perceive situations positively.

As critics have suggested, this new discourse around happiness has sought to redefine it as (a) a consequence of success and (b) the necessary requirement for further success. What is more, people's emotional states are conceptualised as tools to be engaged, employed and placed on the line in order to sculpt the self into a more competitive and effective agent (Sugarman, 2015). Additionally, individuals are *responsible* for their emotional experiences. That is, positive psychology advocates that individuals must learn to accept responsibility for sculpting their emotions into a set of tools that will serve them as they seek to better their lives and experience the resultant emotional flush that success brings. Equally, as Sugarman (2015) has noted, unhappiness is also people's responsibility and tends to be conceptualised as a personal failure to accept responsibility for one's feelings and circumstances and/or to take action. For Sugarman (2015, p. 110), 'the new discourse on happiness reflects a fundamental transformation in how we see life and our relation to it'.

The central concern here is the relationship between psychology and neoliberal governmentality (Foucault, 1991). As discussed above, a significant feature of neoliberal governmentality is the idea that individuals are seduced, persuaded and prompted to cultivate dispositions thought to be correlated with an active pursuit of particular prized goals. Such persuasion relies heavily upon cultural and structural discourse that serves to reward, rationalise and idealise these neoliberal dispositions (Gorz, 1999). However, it should also be noted that this discourse is more persuasive and effectively implemented when it is *legitimised* in the minds of individuals. To this end, some have viewed knowledge construction within academia as a 'technology' in the sense that it can operate to legitimise, insert and embed 'knowledge' that seeks to understand, construct and influence individuals' psyche in ways that best serve neoliberal ends (Binkley, 2011). As Rose (1999, p. 93) astutely suggested, reflected in the psychological sciences is the fact that 'we have entered, it appears, the age of the calculable person, whose individuality is no longer ineffable, unique and beyond knowledge, but can be known, mapped, calibrated, evaluated, quantified, predicted and managed'.

It is concerning, for a myriad of reasons (Giroux, 2002, 2005, 2009; Levidow, 2002; Lyotard, 1984), that the organisational systems and structures within which academic life and work take place have been distorted by a 'business ontology'. As academics change, so does the very nature of the knowledge they produce. Lyotard (1984, pp. 4–5) first noted that knowledge is changing:

> knowledge is and will be produced in order to be sold, it is and will be consumed in order to be valorized in a new production: in both cases, the goal is exchange. Knowledge ceases to be an end in itself, it loses its 'use-value'.

Those producing knowledge too are increasingly servants of the regime of excellence in higher education. It is becoming clear that the knowledge they produce is at risk of being 'hollowed out', devoid of ideology and values that have either personal meaning or fall outside of the parameters of the regime of neoliberal excellence (Butler and Spoelstra, 2014; Cribb and Gerwitz, 2013; Giroux, 2002, 2009; Patrick, 2013).

As academics also come under increasing pressure to construct knowledge that serves the neoliberal agenda, Carr and Batlle (2015) have expressed specific concerns about how psychology might be transformed. That is, what if psychological researchers, themselves under increasing pressure to become 'academic entrepreneurs', begin to ask questions, generate knowledge and develop theory that simply follows a market-driven agenda? *Psychological* theory, knowledge and research, currently preoccupied with calculation, calibration, quantification, prediction, control and management of the individual psyche (Rose, 1999), is a particularly suitable candidate for pursuing a knowledge base that seeks, ultimately, to construct, enable and produce *Homo Economicus*. In this book, I argue that there is a pressing need to take stock of knowledge production in the psychological sciences, particularly where it might serve as a neoliberal rationalisation program or technology of governance. We must be sure that cultivating and enabling the psychological characteristics that support and further the neoliberal agenda do not cost us some of the deeper, spiritually and existentially meaningful aspects of human experience (Wilson, 2008). As Fox, Prilleltensky and Austin (2009, p. 8) have suggested:

> Psychology is not, and cannot be, a neutral endeavour conducted by scientists and practitioners detached from social and political circumstances. It is a human and social endeavour. Psychologists live in specific social contexts. They are influenced by differing interests and complex power dynamics. Mainstream psychologists too often shy away from the resulting moral, social, and political implications.

In their vision for the development of a critical psychology, Fox *et al.* (2009) asked a number of key questions: (a) Does the field promote (wittingly or unwittingly) the status quo in society? (b) Does the field promote social justice or injustice for the population of interest or for society at large? (c) Is there awareness of societal repercussions of knowledge creation and practices, or is the field oblivious to potential negative effects? (d) Do researchers declare their values or assume what they do is value free? As Erica Burman (2008) has noted in *Deconstructing Developmental Psychology*, this means that we must critically engage not only with the knowledge claims that psychology makes, but also with the circumstances in which such knowledge was constructed, the social and political influences that made the topic seem important and the social and political consequences of that research.

Parker (2009) has suggested that the emergence of 'pockets' of critical psychological thought reflects a reluctance to completely ignore political struggles.

Accordingly, some movements in critical psychology combine a theoretical awareness in relation to politics (e.g. an objection to neoliberal society and the various disciplinary practices through which it is reproduced) with the 'practical task of overthrowing it' (Parker, 2009, p. 72). Such thinking reflects a logical position that rationalises the refusal of capitalism, illuminates the plight of those who suffer because of it and aims for disciplinary transformation that places social justice at the heart of conceptual and methodological developments (Parker, 2009).

In relation to educational psychology, Corcoran (2014) has highlighted how the discipline has all too often ignored its relationship with politics and frequently still holds onto a desire to keep politics and science separate. However, recently, critical bodies of work relating strongly to education have interrogated psychology in relation to issues such as the limitations and discriminations in psychometric testing (Danziger, 1990) and, more recently, the medicalisation of childhood (Rafalovich, 2013; Timimi, 2010). For example, compelling research calls our attention to an apparent correlation between political mandates within educational policy and rates of diagnosis of disorders such as attention deficit hyperactivity disorder (ADHD) (Fulton et al., 2009). A cultural context loaded with anxieties surrounding the control of unruly children and an education system in which teachers, parents and children are pressured towards viewing non-conformity to a myopic set of learning practices and behavioural norms as 'pathological' has provided the social platform for the normalisation of concepts such as ADHD (Timimi, 2002, 2010). For critics (Breggin, 2001; Timimi et al., 2004), this has provided the ideal opportunity to project responsibility for the ADHD phenomenon onto individuals and their families in the form of 'psychopathology', drawing attention away from social, cultural and political explanations and social responsibility. Timimi et al. (2004) have argued that the current epidemic of ADHD in the West reflects a profound change in what we expect of our children, coupled with an unwitting alliance between drug companies, some doctors and psychology/psychiatry that has legitimised and normalised the practice of dispensing performance enhancing substances in a crude attempt to subdue current anxieties about children's (particularly boys') development.

Contemporary critics (Martin and McLellan, 2013; Patrick, 2013; Sugarman, 2015) have expressed concern that psychology has played a significant role in transforming and constructing 'ideal students' for the age of neoliberalism. In their book *The Education of Selves: How Psychology Transformed Students*, Martin and McLellan (2013) make a case for the ways in which educational psychology has transformed itself into a discipline that seeks ultimately to conceptualise and develop young people's hypothesised capacities to be rational and strategic managers able to monitor, strategise, reinforce and motivate themselves in pursuit of their own self-interests (Sugarman, 2015). As Sugarman (2015, p. 112) succinctly summarises, in neoliberal society,

> Enterprising students are individuals who come to possess specialized executive skills and strategies adapted instrumentally for optimal performance

in academic and life tasks. Perhaps most centrally, enterprising students develop a view of lifelong learning as an essential tool for remaining competitive in the perpetually changing world of flexible capitalism.

For Martin and McLellan (2013), educational psychology has all too often been a complicit ally in the governance of young people towards specific forms of subjectivity and ways of being that are suited to neoliberal society. What is more, they argue that this has come at the cost of all other conceptualisations of the educative process.

In his recent article 'The McDonaldization of Childhood', Timimi (2010) sketched out a comprehensive critique of the ways in which neoliberal society has fundamentally changed the nature of childhood. There are key issues that, he argued, are a significant risk to children and young people's well-being and he rallied psychology and psychiatry to respond to these challenges.

1. Family structure is undeniably changing. We are witnessing the demise of the extended family, an increase in divorce and separation rates, an increase in parental working hours and a decrease in the amount of time children are able to spend with parents (Timimi, 2010). Eichner (2010) has highlighted the mounting pressure that has been placed on family life and caretaking in American society, where people work increasingly long hours and both mothers and fathers are enticed into the workplace. For Eichner (2010), what is particularly surprising has been the muted political and legal response (in comparison to policy in other countries) to such work-family conflict (i.e. provision of legal and political measures designed to protect family life, provide a platform for familial care-giving and ameliorate work-family conflict). She has argued that such inaction in law and public policy reflects the dominant neoliberal ideology insofar that it fails to acknowledge the importance of dependency in human life and seems to reflect an abandonment of the state's most basic responsibilities, explicitly individualising responsibility for managing and ameliorating work-life conflict.

2. Connected to the above, critics (Crittenden, 2006; England and Folbre, 2006; Hartford, 2010) have expressed concern over a society that measures worth and achievement almost solely in terms of money and normative success (Crittenden, 2006). Hartford (2010) argues that (a) care itself is now bought, sold and routinely offered as a commodity and (b) the nonmarket work of everyday care (particularly in familial contexts) has been explicitly excluded from most economic and political analyses of what matters (England and Folbre, 2006). Consequently, care is increasingly marginalised by policy in contexts where its 'benefits' (in a neoliberal sense) are not explicitly obvious in economic terms.

3. The commercialisation/commodification of childhood has dramatically increased consumer goods, which are specifically targeted at children, and has created new commercial opportunities that are 'located' in childhood. As

examples, Timimi (2010) highlights the 'parenting' industry and the pharmaceutical industry. Advertising and marketing to children have risen dramatically in recent years, and in 2004 were estimated to exceed $15 billion (Schor, 2004). It is difficult to deny that children have become a business opportunity for various sectors of the market.

4 Similarly, critics have argued that 'food marketing' is a major cause of the shift to unhealthy diets dominated by added sugar, fat and salt. They point to the billions of dollars of food advertising and marketing which children are exposed to, on television, in schools, on the internet and in the shops (Nestle, 2002). As Timimi (2010) noted, children's diets now contain higher levels of sugar, saturated fats, salt and chemical additives and lower levels of certain essential fatty acids and fresh fruit and vegetables.

5 Children's lifestyles have been transformed by a decrease in exercise and the 'domestication' of childhood due to moral panics surrounding the 'risks' for children (Timimi, 2010). This has resulted in more indoor pursuits such as computers and TV and has served to accentuate moral panics around the medicalisation of childhood obesity and weight (Murray, 2008).

6 Finally, neoliberal educational policy has fundamentally transformed the nature of the system in which children are educated. In the previous chapter, one of the central points to note about the neoliberal educational landscape was the idea that its key features (e.g. high stakes testing, market values, the knowledge economy, accountability, performativity, the language of managerialism) produce new subjectivities. That is, it has restructured the life world of teachers, academics, children and young people. New identities and personal struggles are literally carved out upon its platform, and it is difficult to deny that all manner of injustices have been created under its reign.

Timimi (2010) has suggested that it is time for those concerned with children's psychological and social well-being to look more closely at the various ways in which the injustices of neoliberal childhoods are manifested and can be combated. Couldry (2008, p. 3) has warned that the 'truths' of neoliberalism 'would be unacceptable if stated openly, even if their consequences unfold before our eyes every day . . . those truths must therefore be translated into an acceptable version of the values and compulsions on which that cruelty depends'. In this book, I argue that psychology is in need of a critical voice that mobilises the tools it has to offer in the struggles that are played out on the neoliberal educational landscape.

The importance of a critical voice

In a recent article supporting the virtues of a space within psychology that prioritises social justice, Louis et al. (2014) pointed out the relative lack of attention that psychology has paid to social justice (especially when compared to sociology). In their exploration of 3.27 million psychology-related articles on APA's PsycNET database, they identified that only 1 per cent of the articles were devoted to the topic of social justice. Furthermore, of these articles the overwhelming majority focused upon justice in relation to practitioners in contexts allied to health care or criminology. That is, there was a distinct inertia in relation to psychological research explicitly addressing and speaking to social justice in a political sense.

Louis et al. (2014) went on to ask whether such a distinct neglect and disproportionate focus (in comparison, almost 10 per cent of articles specifically focused upon 'the brain') on social justice really *should* characterise the landscape of psychological research. They argued that the lack of concern with social justice in psychology reflects what is currently normal and pointed out that societal and disciplinary norms still overwhelmingly position psychology as morally neutral. Furthermore, those who choose to study psychology and pursue it as a career path tend to be exposed to a 'curriculum' that explicitly socialises practitioners and researchers into positivist, individualistic values and tend to think about morality rather narrowly, primarily in terms of ethical conduct (Louis et al., 2014).

The emergence of new groups, identities and voices with differing values and norms within the discipline should not *replace* 'what is'. However, at present, minority groups that tend to prioritise issues related to political and social justice are marginalised and often segregated from the mainstream. For example, as Louis et al. (2014) noted, in the United States the mainstream *American Psychological Association* (APA) currently has around 137,000 members, compared to the 3,000 members of the *Society for the Psychological Study of Social Issues* (yet the latter group is involved in formally lobbying the US government and is represented as an NGO at the United Nations and UN Economic and Social Council). Other small groups include the APA divisions for *Peace and Conflict, Community Research and Action, Religion and Spirituality* and *Theoretical and Philosophical Psychology*. Furthermore, the *Australian Psychological Society* has special interest groups such as *Psychologists for Peace* and *Women and Psychology*, and in Europe (for example) there is the *German Peace Psychology* forum and the UK *Centre for Qualitative and Theoretical Research on the Reproduction and Transformation of Language, Subjectivity and Practice*. At present, one way of viewing the relative minority status of such groups and their separation from the mainstream is that they simply reflect 'the marginalization of social justice concerns and their institutional distance from power' (Louis et al., 2014, p. 21).

However, it is also important to realise that the emergence of such groups and voices is useful in a number of ways. First, they bring to light particular values (e.g. social justice, political conscience) that may previously have been marginal or confined to 'zones of indifference' within the codes of practice of dominant groups. Accordingly, as the norms and values of existing and emerging voices are contested and conflicted, individuals, subgroups and groups are challenged to position themselves in relation to such norms and values (Louis, 2008). The evaluation or choice of a norm, value structure or agenda is ultimately a judgement not only of the degree to which it captures meaningful homogeneity among in-group members but also of heterogeneity from other reference groups. In essence, as Louis et al. (2014) have noted, new norms, codes and values may flourish within certain subgroups (e.g. feminist psychology, critical psychology) because they provide space for diversity and because the very fact that they are different from 'what is' affirms and reinforces how they offer an alternative from the mainstream. In essence, psychology, like politics, *should* be a contested space, where different groups with differing identities and perceptions of justice are constantly evolving and contesting what matters.

Another way of looking at it is that the emergence of new voices can colonise the mainstream. When this is the case, psychologists with different agendas are, for example, able to run for office within mainstream organisations. They can then play a role in defining positions and new ideas by penetrating mainstream institutional bodies, ensuring, for example, that those who are passionate about social justice issues are also a part of producing and reviewing relevant position papers and policy statements in the mainstream (Louis et al., 2014). To illustrate, Fowers (2015) has noted the considerable progress in relation to the efforts made by theoretical psychologists to colonise the APA. Teo's (2009) efforts to take the *Journal of Theoretical and Philosophical Psychology* from a semi-annual Sage publication to a quarterly APA publication is a notable example. Also noteworthy is Slithe's (1993) efforts to take the same journal from a newsletter to a fully fledged academic journal. Such movements are evidence that it is possible for alternative voices to move closer to the mainstream and to ensure that their visibility and respectability is enhanced (Fowers, 2015). For Fowers (2015, p. 8), what is particularly important about such changes for minority voices is that they facilitate the development of an infrastructure 'for pursuing the constitutive goods of theoretical psychology: knowledge, professional identity, communion with our colleagues, and meaningful contributions to our profession'.

Such colonisation opens up the possibility for justice-minded psychologists to initiate and encourage norm changes. As Louis *et al.* (2014) have noted, psychologists prioritising social justice can then capitalise on the opportunity to battle political oppression in and through the domain of science, where they are advantaged by expertise (Harris, 2010) and can utilise psychology's social and political capital (Nicholson, 1998). It is then possible to identify conservative political assumptions outside of the discipline or within it (reflected in research questions, constructs and hypotheses) and attempt to pursue an agenda that falsifies or combats such assumptions. Ultimately, there is much to gain from the emergence of a critical voice that prioritises social justice. In the *Journal of Theoretical and Philosophical Psychology's* special issue on social justice, Louis *et al.* (2014, p. 23) aptly summarise this:

> A social justice view is inherently evangelical – we aspire to spread justice, to achieve social change. But we can do so effectively only by recognizing our views as located in group identities and norms. The questions then become, not how to make other psychologists do what we want, but how to make other psychologists part of our group, and/or how to change their group norm. This is a political, collective project, not a matter of individual chutzpah and choice. The processes by which we are allowed to contest the

relationship of justice and psychology are equally defined by group norms and group identities – here we write journal articles; we are not permitted to use bombs and napalm, nor even targeted assassinations of our rivals.

Developing a critical voice

As psychologists who seek to position social and political justice at the forefront of knowledge production and academic inquiry, it is important to reflect upon how we might colonise and contribute to the mainstream. Fowers (2015) has recently provided a framework delineating the important functions of a critical and theoretical voice in psychology. Specifically, his framework outlines four key functions: *research*, *reflection*, *re-examination* and *reformulation*.

1. *Research* does not refer to the empirical type. This function refers to intimately researching and understanding the psychological theory, knowledge base and practice upon which we seek to *reflect*. For example, in order to comprehensively understand and appreciate how social and political justice might apply or relate to research and knowledge in a given area, it is important that we fully grasp the central constructs, assumptions and hypotheses.
2. Subsequently, critical and theoretical *reflection* and *re-examination* are essential. These functions refer to the critical questioning of assumptions, methods, interpretations, judgements and hypotheses. Fowers (2015) has noted that theoretical and critical psychology have developed powerful tools that help us to reveal and analyse the 'blind spots, ideologies, and unacknowledged moral commitments in psychology' (p. 5). Such critical analysis is highly important to psychology because the discipline cannot claim to be reflective, progressive and just without it.
3. In the end, research, reflection and critique with social and political justice in mind, are of little benefit if they are not converted into disciplinary transformation. *Reformulation*, the final function forwarded by Fowers (2015), is particularly important because it extends the work of critical and theoretical psychology beyond critique, offering genuine alternatives and theoretical development. It is important to note that reformulation is a difficult and lengthy challenge that takes time. For Fowers (2015), this is because (a) reformulation is an aspirational goal that requires significant research, reflection and re-examination and often involves periods of floundering and flailing in the dark and (b) quite simply, excellent contributions in theoretical psychology, like anything else, always take time. Nonetheless, as Fowers (2015) noted in his review, there have been significant reformulations that the field of theoretical psychology can be proud of (Fowers, 2012; Richardson, 2012; Slife, 2004).

In this book, I argue that colonising the mainstream with a voice that prioritises social justice is something that can happen in the discipline as a whole – but also *within* individual psychological theories. Within individual theories, it is important to encourage and foster a space that places the sort of reflection, re-examination and reformulation outlined by Fowers (2015) at the core of its agenda. First, this will require careful critique of current knowledge, assumptions, values and methods allied to individual frameworks, especially as they relate to issues of social and political justice and political ideology. For the most part, psychological theories are 'organised' bodies of knowledge and ideas. They tend to be organised around particular key constructs and lines of inquiry that reflect dominant discourses, language, themes and codes of conduct. As Carr and Batlle (2015) noted, where the dominant discourse and research themes allied to a given theoretical framework have not explicitly started out with social and political justice in mind, it is often the case that our frameworks and research avenues contain many blind spots that have significant implications for justice.

In their recent discussion of this issue in the theoretical and philosophical psychology literature, Carr and Batlle (2015) demonstrated how careful reflection and re-examination of key constructs, assumptions and specific research avenues allied to particular theoretical frameworks frequently reveal blind spots in relation to issues of social justice in neoliberal society. As the researchers noted in this paper, revealing and reflecting upon these blind spots can help us to appreciate (a) the ways in which our own assumptions, lines of inquiry, constructs and theoretical discourse often fail to recognise or unwittingly serve what might be considered an oppressive neoliberal agenda and (b) the ways in which our theoretical language, tools, constructs and knowledge base might better align with and contribute to social justice in neoliberal society (were we to develop a theoretical space that prioritised it). Clearly, within each of our theories, this involves reflecting upon how our questions, assumptions, hypotheses and data might better reflect a quest for knowledge that rationalises the refusal of unjust systems, illuminates the plight of those who suffer because of them and aims for disciplinary transformation that places social justice at the heart of conceptual and methodological developments (Carr and Batlle, 2015; Fowers, 2015; Louis *et al.*, 2014; Parker, 2009).

The neoliberal educational landscape is rife with all manner of injustices. One might choose to focus upon the inner lives of the 'new performative teachers' deeply struggling with inner conflict that arises when they seek to portray a veneer of professional excellence to which they are held accountable, 'performing' in ways that feel inauthentic and morally wrong (Ball, 2003). Or, the ways in which high stakes testing is corrupting our education system (Nichols and Berliner, 2008), 'persuading' millions of children, young people, families, teachers and schools that their worth is based upon the extent to which they deviate from an increasingly myopic version of excellence that is rooted in the needs of an emerging oligarchy (Saltman, 2000). Or, perhaps one might focus upon the demoralising ways that higher education has been 'hollowed out' (Cribb and Gerwitz, 2013), persuading academics, ever more pervasively, to produce knowledge that is one-dimensional, uncritical and personally irrelevant (Butler and Spoelstra, 2014) and dampening their motivation and enthusiasm for what they do (Wilkesmann and Schmid, 2014).

Whichever way we turn, there are multiple problems that might reflect starting points for psychological inquiry that is rooted in social justice. Exploring and addressing these lines of inquiry does not mean that psychologists allied to established schools of thought, theoretical frameworks and research traditions must abandon the constructs, concepts and methods they know in search of social justice. As Louis *et al.* (2014) have noted,

> We may seize the opportunity, where oppressive discourses lay claim to publicly verifiable 'natural' facts, to battle our political opponents in the domain in which we are advantaged by our 'expertise' (Harris, 2010). We may exploit our position to identify conservative political propositions that are empirical hypotheses. When these hypotheses are falsifiable, and false, we can pursue a political social justice agenda through positivism: that is, by falsifying the conservatives' claims.

Hence, it is not the case, as some have suggested (Prilleltensky and Walsh-Bowers, 1993), that our existing tools, constructs and knowledge, while perhaps not explicitly developed with social justice in mind, cannot be helpful. On the other hand, however, as Fowers (2015) suggested, we should take every opportunity to critically research and critique our dominant constructs, assumptions and ideas, being open to how they might be shaped, transformed and further developed in accordance with socially just lines of inquiry. The above will take time, discussion, critique, deliberation (something that is increasingly marginalised by the pressure on academics to produce quickly available, made-to-order knowledge) and a willingness to engage with and synthesise literature from broader disciplines (such as sociology, politics and cultural studies) where the injustices of neoliberal society have been more significantly developed and analysed. My intention in this book is to begin this process of research, reflection and re-examination with particular reference to key theoretical frameworks allied to motivation in the context of education.

Motivational theory: developing a critical space

> Regardless of social strata or cultural origin, examples of both children and adults who are apathetic, alienated, and irresponsible are abundant. Such non-optimal human functioning can be observed not only in our psychological clinics but also among the millions who, for hours a day, sit passively before their televisions, stare blankly from the back of their classrooms, or wait listlessly for the weekend as they go about their jobs. The persistent, proactive, and positive tendencies of human nature are clearly not invariantly apparent.
> (Ryan and Deci, 2000, p. 68)

In the above quote, Ryan and Deci (2000) encapsulate the central role occupied by motivation in human life and offer an appreciation as to why the development of understanding in relation to human motivation clearly matters. Ryan (2012) has suggested that motivation is being more intensively studied today than ever before. To account for this, he offers three explanations: (1) the theoretical depth and interdisciplinary nature of motivation studies, (2) methodological innovation (such as new statistical and experimental advances) and (3) the practical importance of motivational science for contemporary society. In relation to the third explanation, he notes that there has been renewed appreciation for motivation as a science because it has become simply obvious that motivation matters 'for productivity at work, learning in schools, and adherence within clinics' (Ryan, 2012, p. 9). That is, motivational science offers significant insight into how important and valued societal goals might be actualised.

Perhaps unsurprisingly, Ryan's (2012) portrayal of motivational science explicitly acknowledges the main contribution of its theoretical models as one that relates to issues of 'practical prediction and control':

> Psychological models of motivation . . . operate on the level of inferred constructs, intended to capture the forces at work in energizing and directing action. Causal models at this level of analysis can be a particularly important point of entry into describing and predicting motivated behaviors. If one wants to intervene in intentional behaviors (e.g., dietary habits, work practices, physical activity and exercise), knowing the types of feedback, meanings, significant cognitions, and perceived social contexts that support or thwart these behaviors provides considerable leverage. (Ryan, 2012, p. 5)

One way of interpreting this quote (particularly through the use of words such as 'intervention' and 'leverage') is the assumption that the role of motivational science is (at least partially) to help unravel a key dimension of a computable person, whose psyche can be broken down, calibrated, evaluated, quantified, predicted and controlled in the ways described by Rose (1999).

How should motivation researchers think about the 'apathy', 'lack of engagement', 'irresponsibility' and 'non-optimal human functioning' attributed to young people in Ryan and Deci's (2000) quote above? What is the aim of the study of human motivation in relation to issues that may be deeply politically and socially rooted? Does motivational science implicitly (and perhaps unwittingly) start from the assumption that it should create a program of rationality that aims to know, map, predict and manage individuals' motivational dispositions towards particular behavioural (political) ends? If so, to what extent might the theories, assumptions, questions and knowledge that emerge from such a project reflect 'technologies of governance', playing their role in the shaping and sculpting subjectivities that serve to ensure that individuals function 'non-apathetically' and 'optimally' within and towards particular value systems?

What if the science of motivation sought to rationalise the refusal of 'what is', illuminating the plight of those who suffer because of de-motivating social, political and school level practices, aiming for disciplinary transformation that places social justice at the heart of its theoretical, methodological and intellectual project? This book is a first attempt to bring social justice more firmly into the realms of motivational science in the context of education. It is an attempt to realise, encourage and foster an alternative space within motivational psychology in education by mobilising the 'goods' of theoretical and critical psychology (reflection, re-examination and reformulation) (Fowers, 2015). At present, dominant theories of motivation in the field of social psychology are highly established, organised bodies of knowledge that have emerged around key constructs, questions, assumptions, traditions and methods. In social psychology, these bodies of knowledge have tended to adopt the value neutrality that is typical of the discipline. They have not tended to develop with social justice as a starting point.

The knowledge base that has emerged in motivational theory to date may, upon careful reflection and consideration, have much to offer the debate surrounding the neoliberalisation of education. We might also seek to reformulate the architecture of our theories (reflected in the questions we ask, assumptions we make and knowledge we construct) so that it also encompasses knowledge that clearly rationalises the refusal of unjust value systems and places social justice at heart of its developments (Carr and Batlle, 2015; Fowers, 2015; Louis et al., 2014; Parker, 2009). In the pages that follow, I seek to critically explore the interface between neoliberal educational policy and motivational theory. For expedience, discussions are confined to two theoretical frameworks that have been highly popular in the study of motivation in education: achievement goal theory and self-determination theory.

Goal theory has been one of the most prominent theories of motivation in educational research for more than twenty-five years (Senko et al., 2011). However, recently, theorists have discussed the challenges, controversies and need for new directions that confront the field. As Senko et al. (2011, p. 36) have expressed:

> How should we proceed, given the theoretical and empirical progress thus far? . . . We believe a more fruitful and progressive research agenda . . . would build on theoretical refinements and research findings discussed . . . and, hopefully, move past the old debates.

In response to Senko et al.'s (2011) call, if goal theory is currently at a crossroads then it may be that the theory has reached a critical moment in its evolution. Perhaps this is an opportune time to ensure that the future shape of our research questions and theoretical refinement is guided not only by the research avenues that have been carved out to date but also by new avenues that emerge when we pragmatically consider our ideas in the context of burning issues related to social justice currently facing education.

Alongside goal theory, self-determination theory has made a significant contribution to the development of understanding about human motivation in education. As Ryan and Deci (2000) have pointed out, the theory has offered education a rich framework that posits that social contextual conditions that can support the key human needs for feelings of competence, autonomy and relatedness are the basis for the development of intrinsic motivation, more self-determined forms of extrinsic motivation and associated well-being. Furthermore, they have noted, the facilitation of more self-determined learning in schools requires classroom conditions that allow satisfaction of these three basic human needs – 'that is that support the innate needs to feel connected, effective, and agentic as one is exposed to new ideas and exercises new skills' (Ryan and Deci, 2000, p. 65).

Recent lines of thinking in self-determination theory (Wilkesmann and Schmid, 2014) have begun to consider the theory's potential to contribute to broader debate and critique of the changing nature of education. For example, in the context of the neoliberalisation of higher education in Germany, Wilkesmann and Schmid (2014) recognised the potential incompatibility between the corporatisation of higher education practice (e.g. performance-related pay and budgeting, a culture of performativity and accountability) and the development of intrinsic motivation in academics. The study used self-determination theory as its framework and concluded:

> Rectorates are well advised to save monetary funds by implementing and emphasizing symbolic rewards and protecting the professoriate's demand for autonomy against all these highly ineffective 'management fads' in higher education . . . NPM [New Performance Management] tools run the risk of reducing and harming internalized teaching motivation in the long run . . . NPM may be successful in the re-structuring of higher education institutions into a 'complete organization' . . . but NPM causes rather significant unintended effects on the micro-level of the professors' behavior, which outweigh the benefits of this organizational management reform. (pp. 20–21)

It is encouraging that researchers are beginning to recognise that motivational theory might have a significant contribution to make in rationalising the refusal of the forces that threaten education and illuminating the plight of those facing the struggle (Parker, 2009). In this sense, there is reason for optimism in relation to the emergence of a genuine critical space in educational motivational psychology.

References

American Psychological Association. (2010). *Ethical Principles of Psychologists and Code of Conduct*. Washington, DC: Author.

Ball, S. (2003). The teacher's soul and the terrors of performativity. *Journal of Educational Policy*, 18(2), 215–28.

Binkley, S. (2011). Happiness, positive psychology and the program of neoliberal governmentality. *Subjectivity*, 4(4), 371–94.

Bourdieu, P. (December 1998). The essence of neoliberalism, translated by Jeremy J. Shapiro, *Le Monde diplomatique*. Available at http://mondediplo.com/1998/12/08bourdieu.

Breggin, P.R. (2001). *Talking Back to Ritalin: What Doctors Aren't Telling You About Stimulants and ADHD* (Revised). Cambridge: Perseus Books.

British Psychological Society. (2009). *Code of Ethics and Conduct*. Leicester, UK: Author.
Burman, E. (2008). *Deconstructing Developmental Psychology*. London: Brunner-Routledge.
Butler, N. and Spoelstra, S. (2014). The Regime of Excellence and the Erosion of Ethos in Critical Management Studies. *British Journal of Managemement*, *25*(3), 538–50.
Canadian Psychological Association. (2008). *Canadian Code of Ethics for Psychologists* (3rd edn). Ottawa, ON: Author.
Carr, S. and Batlle, I.C. (2015). Attachment theory, neoliberalism, and social conscience. *Journal of Theoretical and Philosophical Psychology*, *35*(3), 160–76.
Corcoran, T. (2014). Heterotopics: Learning as second nature. In T. Corcoran (ed.), *Psychology in Education: Critical Theory~Practice* (pp. 37–52). Rotterdam: Sense Publisher.
Couldry, N. (2008). Reality TV, or the secret theatre of neoliberalism. *Review of Education, Pedagogy, and Cultural Studies*, *30*(3), 3–13.
Cribb, A. and Gewirtz, S. (2013). The hollowed-out university? A critical analysis of changing institutional and academic norms in UK higher education. *Discourse*, *34*(3), 338–50.
Crittenden, A. (2006). How mothers' work disappeared. In A. Wharton (ed.), *Working in America: Continuity, Conflict, and Change* (pp. 18–31). New York: McGraw Hill.
Danziger, K. (1990). *Constructing the Subject: Historical Origins of Psychological Research*. Cambridge, MA: Cambridge University Press.
Eichner, M. (2010). Families, human dignity, and state support for caretaking: Why the united states' failure to ameliorate the work-family conflict is a dereliction of the government's basic responsibilities, *North Carolina Law Review*, *8*, 1593–1598.
England, P. and Folbre, N. (2006). Capitalism and the erosion of care. In A. Wharton (ed.), *Working in America: Continuity, Conflict, and Change* (pp. 495–510). New York: McGraw Hill.
Foucault, M. (1991). Governmentality. In G. Burchell, C. Gordon and P. Miller (eds), *The Foucault Effect: Studies in Governmentality* (pp. 87–104). Hemel Hempstead: Harvester Wheatsheaf.
Foucault, M. (2008). *The Birth of Biopolitics: Lectures at the Collège de France, 1978–1979*, translated by G. Burchell. In A.I. Davidson, (ed.), New York: Palgrave Macmillan.
Fowers, B.J. (2015). The promise of a flourishing theoretical psychology. *Journal of Theoretical and Philosophical Psychology*, *35*, 145–59.
Fox, D., Prilleltensky, I. and Austin, S. (2009). Critical psychology for social justice: concerns and dilemmas. In D. Fox, I. Prilleltensky and S. Austin (eds), *Critical Psychology: An Introduction* (pp. 3–20). London: Sage.
Fulton, B.D., Scheffler, R.M., Hinshaw, S.P., Levine, P., Stone, S., Brown, T.T. and Modrek, S. (2009). National variation of ADHD diagnostic prevalence and medication use: Health care providers and education policies. *Psychiatric Services*, *60*(8), 1075–1083.
Giroux, H.A. (2002). Neoliberalism, corporate culture, and the promise of higher education: The university as a democratic public sphere. *Harvard Educational Review*, *72*(4), 425–63.
Giroux, H.A. (2005). The terror of neoliberalism: Rethinking the significance of cultural politics. *College Literature*, *32*(1), 1–19.
Giroux, H.A. (2009). Education and the crisis of youth: Schooling and the promise of democracy. *The Educational Forum*, *73*(1), 8–18.
Gore, A. (2010). *Bluebird: Women and the New Psychology of Happiness*. New York: Farrar, Straus, and Giroux.
Gorz, A. (1999). *Reclaiming Work*. London: Pluto.
Hamann, T. (2009). Neoliberalism, governmentality, and ethics. *Foucault Studies*, *6*, 37–59.
Harris, S. (2010). *The Moral landscape: How Science Can Determine Human Values*. New York: Free Press.

Hartford, I. (2010). My work Utopia: Pursuing a satisfactory work life amid an alienating world. *Human Architecture: Journal of the Sociology of Self-Knowledge*, 8, 167–76.

Levidow, L. (2002). Marketizing higher education: Neoliberal strategies and counter-strategies. In K. Robins and F. Webster (eds), *The Virtual University? Knowledge, Markets and Management* (pp. 227–48). Oxford, UK: Oxford University Press.

Louis, W.R. (2008). Intergroup positioning and power. In F.M. Moghaddam, R. Harré and N. Lee (eds), *Global Conflict Resolution Through Positioning Analysis* (pp. 21–39). New York: Springer.

Louis, W.R., Mavor, K.I., La Macchia, S.T. and Amiot, C.E. (2014). Social justice and psychology: What is and what should be. *Journal of Theoretical and Philosophical Psychology*, 34(1), 14–27.

Lyotard, J.F. (1984). *The Postmodern Condition: A Report on Knowledge*, (Vol. 10). Manchester: Manchester University Press.

Martin, J. and McLellan, A. (2013). *The Education of Selves: How Psychology Transformed Students*. New York: Oxford University Press.

Murray, S. (2008). Pathologizing 'fatness': Medical authority and popular culture. *Sociology of Sport Journal*, 25(1), 7–21.

Nestle, M. (2002). *Food Politics: How the Food Industry Influences Nutrition and Health*. Berkeley, CA: University of California Press.

Nichols, S.L. and Berliner, D.C. (2008). Why has high-stakes testing so easily slipped into contemporary American life? *Phi Delta Kappan*, 89(9), 672–676.

Nicholson, I.A.M. (1998). Ethics, objectivity, and professional authority. *American Psychologist*, 53(3), 321–22.

Parker, I. (2009). Critical psychology and revolutionary marxism. *Theory and Psychology*, 19(1), 71–92.

Patrick, F. (2013). Neoliberalism, the knowledge economy, and the learner: Challenging the inevitability of the commodified self as an outcome of education. *International Scholarly Research Network: Education*, 2013, 8.

Prilleltensky, I. and Walsh-Bowers, R. (1993). Psychology and the moral imperative. *Journal of Theoretical and Philosophical Psychology*, 13(2), 90–102.

Rafalovich, A. (2013). Attention deficit-hyperactivity disorder as the medicalisation of childhood: Challenges from and for sociology. *Sociology Compass*, 7, 343–54.

Richardson, F.C. (2012). On psychology and virtue ethics. *Journal of Theoretical and Philosophical Psychology*, 32, 24–34.

Rose, N. (1999). *Governing the Soul: The Shaping of the Private Self* (2nd edn). London, UK: Free Association Books.

Ryan, R.M. (2012). Motivation, and the organization of human behavior: Three reasons for the reemergence of a field. In R. M. Ryan (ed.), *Oxford Handbook of Human Motivation* (pp. 3–13). Oxford, UK: Oxford University Press.

Ryan, R.M. and Deci, E.L. (2000). Self-determination theory and the facilitation of intrinsic motivation, social development, and well-being. *American Psychologist*, 55(1), 68–78.

Saltman, K. (2000). *Collateral Damage: Corporatizing Public Schools – A Threat to Democracy*. Lanham, ML: Rowman & Littlefield.

Schor, J. (2004). *Born to Buy: The Commercialized Child and the New Consumer Culture*. New York: Scribner.

Senko, C., Hulleman, C.S. and Harackiewicz, J.M. (2011). Achievement goal theory at the crossroads: Old controversies, current challenges, and new directions. *Educational Psychologist*, 46(1), 26–47.

Slife, B.D. (1993). We're a journal! *Journal of Theoretical and Philosophical Psychology*, 13(1), 1.

Slife, B.D. (2004). Taking practice seriously: Toward a relational ontology. *Journal of Theoretical and Philosophical Psychology, 24*, 97–115.

Sugarman, J. (2015). Neoliberalism and psychological ethics. *Journal of Theoretical and Philosophical Psychology, 35*(2), 103–116.

Teo, T. (2009). Editorial. *Journal of Theoretical and Philosophical Psychology,* 29(2), 1–4.

Timimi, S. (2002). *Pathological Child Psychiatry and the Medicalization of Childhood.* London, UK: Brunner-Routledge.

Timimi, S. (2010). The McDonaldization of childhood: Children's mental health in neoliberal market cultures. *Transcultural Psychology, 47*(5), 686–706.

Timimi, S. and 33 co-endorsers (2004). A critique of the international consensus statement on ADHD. *Clinical Child and Family Psychology Review,* 7, 59–63.

Wilkesmann, U. and Schmid, C. (2014). Intrinsic and internalised modes of teaching motivation. *Evidence-Based HRM, 2*(1), 6–27.

Wilson, E. (2008). *Against Happiness: In Praise of Melancholy.* New York: Farrar, Straus, and Giroux.

Wright Mills, C. (1959). *The Sociological Imagination.* New York: Oxford University Press.

3
DISCUSSING GOAL THEORY AND CONTEMPORARY EDUCATIONAL POLICY

Recent papers (Anderman, 2011; Anderman *et al.*, 2010; Patrick *et al.*, 2011) have discussed the importance of the connection between educational psychology, policy and practice. As Patrick *et al.* (2011, p. 75) have pointed out, '... this concern is hardly new ... educational psychologists must truly understand educational contexts and situate their work clearly within them, rather than viewing schools or classrooms just as sites where psychological principles play out'. Patrick *et al.*'s (2011) paper focused upon three important ways that educational psychology might connect with policy and practice: (1) by highlighting the relevance of educational psychology research for educators (i.e. addressing the disconnect between research and practitioners' needs and concerns), (2) by developing collaborative relationships and shared visions with teacher educators (i.e. a need to be proactive in forming relationships with colleagues in other areas of teacher education and softening resistance to the field) and (3) by producing evidence of the benefits of educational psychologists' involvement in teacher education (i.e. demonstrate that teachers benefit from learning about educational psychology). These arguments are examples of how educational psychology has clearly reflected upon its utility in relation to real-world policy and practice.

Nonetheless, explicit recognition of the links between educational psychology and the neoliberal educational landscape has been muted. In relation to Patrick *et al.*'s (2011) first aim, strong appreciation and acknowledgement of the neoliberal platform upon which educational life takes place and of the challenges it creates for individuals would seem to be important. The previous chapters in this book sought to illuminate the struggles that children, young people, teachers and academics face against a backdrop of neoliberal educational policy and practice. They also sought to highlight the need for a critical space in psychology that aims to rationalise the refusal of injustice in the contemporary educational climate. In this chapter, I hope to demonstrate how careful and critical research, reflection and re-examination (Fowers, 2015) of our theoretical frameworks is needed to help us better appreciate how these frameworks might contribute to neoliberal critique in education. As we critically engage with the ways in which neoliberal educational policy is oppressive and unjust, illuminating the plight of those who suffer because of it, we will be able to explore how our theoretical constructs, language and knowledge might challenge some of the dominant assumptions behind such policy (Parker, 2009). Furthermore, we might develop a greater awareness of how our theories might unwittingly contribute to oppression or of how the quest for knowledge in our specific research area might be steered in directions that better contribute to social and political justice. As Fowers (2015) has noted, this cannot be accomplished without careful consideration of our theories, assumptions, research avenues, constructs, knowledge and methods, in relation to educational policy, oppression and injustice.

I begin by focusing upon achievement goal theory. Goal theory has been one of the most popular theories of motivation in educational research for around thirty years (Senko *et al.*, 2011). Recently, theorists have discussed the challenges, controversies and need for new directions that confront the field. As Senko *et al.* (2011, p. 36) pointed out:

> How should we proceed, given the theoretical and empirical progress thus far? . . . We believe a more fruitful and progressive research agenda . . . would build on theoretical refinements and research findings discussed . . . and, hopefully, move past the old debates.

Maehr and Zusho (2009, p. 94) have contended that goal theory ' has remained mostly silent about burning issues facing the field of education' and that 'if the framework is to remain vital and fruitful this trend cannot continue'. In the pages that follow, I contend that a more pragmatic posture in relation to the burning issues facing education may play a useful role in guiding the evolution of goal theory. The chapter begins with an overview of goal theory, before critically discussing the interface with various features of neoliberal educational policy.

An overview of goal theory

Achievement goal approaches to the study of motivation afford competence a central role in the understanding of motivation. The psychological importance of competence-related cognition, affect and behaviour has been well established (Dweck and Elliot, 1983; Elliot and Dweck, 2005), and competence has been identified as a fundamental human need (Deci and Ryan, 1990; White, 1959), the satisfaction of which has been theorised to energise much of everyday thought, feeling and behaviour. Achievement goals have been defined as the purpose, or cognitive-dynamic focus, of competence-related behaviour (Maehr, 1989). As the literature has evolved, different theorists have used slightly different nomenclature and a number of models have been advanced (Ames, 1992; Dweck and Leggett,

1988; Elliot, 1997; Elliot and McGregor, 2001; Harackiewicz *et al.*, 1998; Maehr and Midgley, 1991; Nicholls, 1984; Pintrich, 2000) with different interpretations regarding the antecedents, definition, nature and number of achievement goals. For this reason, Elliot (2005) has suggested, researchers referring to the general overarching conceptual ideas that unite these various achievement goal 'theories' might be advised to point out that they are referring to a general 'achievement goal approach'. Readers should note that this brief overview sought only to outline the cornerstone conceptual assumptions of the theory and the main theoretical developments that have characterised the literature to date. Later in the paper, some of these areas are further unpacked and discussed in the context of the theory-policy arguments raised.

The predominant focus of 'achievement goal approaches' has emanated from the idea that achievement goals reflect how individuals construe competence in a given situation or context (Ames, 1984; Dweck, 1986; Dweck and Leggett, 1988; Elliot, 1997; Nicholls, 1984, 1989). Endorsing *mastery goals* (sometimes labelled *task involved* or *learning goals*), individuals essentially focus themselves on the development and demonstration of competence via personal improvement, self-development and learning. Elliott and Dweck (1988) have suggested that such individuals are essentially concerned with the question 'How can I best acquire this skill or master this task'? In contrast, *performance goals* (sometimes referred to as *ego involved goals*) centre around a focus on the demonstration or proving of competence levels (or the avoidance of incompetence) relative to normative or other-referenced standards. When performance goals are salient, individuals are essentially concerned about demonstrating success (or avoiding failure) by securing a favourable comparison of their ability with that of others.

It has been suggested that such achievement goals provide the framework within which individuals interpret and react to achievement experiences, and they have been implicated in evoking qualitatively different patterns of cognition, affect and behaviour (Ames and Archer, 1988; Dweck and Leggett, 1988; Elliott and Dweck, 1988; Nicholls, 1989). Mastery goal models have tended to predict that a generally adaptive pattern of outcomes is associated with mastery goals and a less adaptive pattern is associated with performance goals (Ames, 1992; Dweck and Leggett, 1988; Pintrich and Schunk, 1996). A large body of research has provided consistent support for this prediction, with mastery goals being associated with adaptive responses in relation to an array of significant cognitive, affective and behavioural outcome variables such as the interpretation of effort, reaction to failure, task choice, intrinsic motivation, affective patterns, and anxiety and performance goals associated with a less adaptive pattern of responses (it is beyond the scope of this article to provide a thorough overview; for a review see Ames, 1992; Dweck and Leggett, 1988; Duda and Hall, 2001; Pintrich and Schunk, 1996; Urdan, 1997). Despite this, there have been notable controversies in the literature relating to (for example) the fact that mastery goals have consistently been unrelated to academic achievement (Hulleman *et al.*, 2010) or that certain manifestations of mastery goals (such as a focus on mastery avoidance) may be detrimental to cognition, affect and behaviour (Sideridis, 2008).

One line of thinking has seen researchers devote attention to goal frameworks incorporating a distinction between 'approach' and 'avoidance' conceptualisations of goals (Elliot and Church, 1997; Elliot and Harackiewicz, 1996; Elliot and McGregor, 2001; Middleton and Midgley, 1997). For example, Elliot's (1997) trichotomous achievement goal framework defined mastery goals in a similar manner to traditional dichotomous goal models (Dweck, 1986; Nicholls, 1984) but segregated performance goals into performance-approach and performance-avoidance categories. According to this framework, individuals focused upon performance-approach goals concern themselves with demonstrating their superior competence levels relative to others, whereas individuals who are focused on performance-avoidance goals attempt to avoid appearing inadequate and demonstrating incompetence relative to others. The bifurcation of the performance goal construct has generated some controversy by providing data to suggest that while performance-avoidance goals are consistently linked to maladaptive outcomes and patterns of learning (Carr, 2006; Elliot and Harackiewicz, 1996; Middleton and Midgley, 1997; Skaalvik, 1997; Wolters, 2004), performance-approach goals have provided less consistent results, being linked to positive outcomes in *some* studies (Elliot and McGregor, 1999; Midgley *et al.*, 1996). Elliot and McGregor (2001) further extended this model to include an additional bifurcation of mastery goals, incorporating *mastery-approach* and *mastery-avoidance* goal distinctions into a 2x2 model. Within this framework, mastery-approach goals reflect a focus on striving to achieve improvement, personal progression and learning. Mastery-avoidance goals are conceptualised as a focus upon striving to avoid *failing to* demonstrating mastery (i.e. *avoiding* learning failures, task mastery and/or improvement) and have been associated in the literature with negative learning outcomes such as high anxiety, negative emotionality and disengagement (Sideridis, 2008; Van Yperen *et al.*, 2009). Goals within this 2x2 framework have been theorised as the underlying dispositional motives of the need to achieve and the need to avoid failure (Atkinson, 1957; McClelland, 1951); the influence of these higher order motives channelled through representational achievement goals. That is, achievement goals have been viewed 'as "focused needs", . . . concretized "servants" of their higher order achievement relevant motives' (Elliot and Church, 1997, p.219). Ultimately, as Senko *et al.* (2011) have summarised, research in the context of the 2x2 model has teased out the idea that *avoidance* manifestations of both mastery *and* performance goals seem to be undesirable frameworks for learning and optimal motivation.

Discussions around *multiple goal* endorsement have devoted attention to understanding not only the strength of endorsement of goals (and their independent effects) but also the abstract ways in which individuals pursue such goals and the relationships that the goals share with each other. In an insightful discussion of multiple goal pursuit in education, Barron and Harackiewicz (2001) discussed the ways in which multiple goals might relate to each other in order to drive individuals' motivational experiences. They forwarded an *interactive* hypothesis suggesting that

Discussing goal theory 63

pursuit of both mastery *and* performance goals would result in more positive effects on particular outcomes, because both goals would be independently advantageous in relation to the outcome. In support of this, for example, studies (Bouffard *et al.*, 1995; Wentzel, 1993) have identified that the most positive effect on grades comes from endorsement of both mastery *and* performance goals. Alternatively, a *specialised* goal hypothesis suggests that goals are likely to have unique effects on different outcomes. For example, mastery goals might be positive predictors of interest (but not of grade level), whereas performance goals might be positive predictors of grade level (but not of interest) (Harackiewicz *et al.*, 1997, 2000). Finally, Barron and Harackiewicz (2001) also proposed a *selective* hypothesis, where pursuit of multiple goals might also require 'the wisdom to know which goal to adopt and when' (Harackiewicz *et al.*, 1997, p. 1293). For example, different achievement goals might be better pursued at different times and students might 'switch between' goals in accordance with which goal is most advantageous at a given time or in a given context. Other studies (Carr, 2006) have investigated the possibility of a *dampening* effect, where (for example) simultaneous pursuit of performance goals seems to dampen the positive effects of mastery goals on a given outcome. Carr's (2006) study did not provide support for this hypothesis, suggesting that a positive association between mastery goals and an array of outcome variables (e.g. intrinsic motivation, positive and negative affect) was not negatively (or positively) affected by simultaneous endorsement of performance approach or avoidance goals (or both). Other researchers, however, have provided support for the dampening perspective (Meece and Holt, 1993; Pintrich and Garcia, 1991). Of the multiple goal approach to investigating goal constructs, Senko *et al.* (2011, p. 30) have suggested that it '. . . departed from the traditional mastery goal perspective that pitted mastery goals against performance goals in an either-or framework'.

There is evidence to support the idea that adoption of goal frameworks and associated motivational responses are significantly linked to social and cultural milieu (Ames and Archer, 1988; Biddle, 2001; Kaplan *et al.*, 2002; Urdan and Turner, 2005). At the classroom level, goal theorists (Ames, 1992; Ames and Archer, 1988; Covington and Omelich, 1984; Epstein, 1988; Maehr and Midgley, 1996) have suggested that classroom goal structures encourage the adoption of specific achievement goals by emphasising and transmitting an environmental goal structure that is made salient through the instructional practices and general messages teachers convey to students. For example, in their classic work, Ames (1992) and Epstein (1988) each identified structural features such as the nature and design of classroom learning activities, evaluation practices, the nature and use of rewards, and the distribution of authority as significant building blocks that (depending upon how they are employed) make salient mastery- or performance-oriented goal structures in the classroom. Although less developed than the literature on personal achievement goals, the predictive utility of classroom goal structures has been fairly well established, with mastery-oriented classroom cultures being strongly linked to positive motivational and psychological development in students and performance-oriented cultures linked to a more maladaptive set of outcomes (for detailed reviews, see Kaplan *et al.*, 2002; Linnenbrink, 2004; Meece *et al.*, 2006; Pintrich and Schunk, 2002; Urdan and Turner, 2005). Research has also linked the predictive utility of these structural representations of achievement goals to contextual emphasis that might emanate from an array of relationship referents, such as parents, peers and teachers (Carr, 2006; Carr and Weigand, 2001; Morris and Kavussanu, 2008; Papaioannou *et al.*, 2008). Conceptually, this avenue of research has also given rise to considerations about the potential consequences of incongruence between goals at various structural levels of representation. For example, researchers (Biddle, 2001; Carr and Weigand, 2008; Linnenbrink, 2005; Linnenbrink and Pintrich, 2001) have investigated (a) a *buffering hypothesis* (where a *personal* mastery orientation might buffer the negative effects of *classroom* performance goals *or* classroom mastery goals might buffer the negative effects of personal performance goals) and (b) a *matching hypothesis* (where classroom contexts that are congruent with students' personal goals are most beneficial as they support personal goal pursuits).

Is high stakes testing a policy-level representation of goals?

Let us begin by pointing out, as Pintrich (2000) noted, that achievement goals simply reflect *values* and *beliefs* in relation to the meaning of achievement and the criteria used to evaluate success. Of course, these values and beliefs need not only be internalised, emphasised and represented at the level of the individual but can also be structurally represented and reflected in cultural practices, as research into goals at the level of the classroom environment has shown (Ames, 1992; Ames and Archer, 1988; Epstein, 1988). Recently, Murayama and Elliot (2009) called for a more considered examination of goals at the structural level of representation, arguing that this might result in a more 'comprehensive portrait of achievement motivation' (p. 443). While they were not explicitly referring to *policy-level* structural representation of achievement goal constructs, there is much to be gained from expanding our understanding of how the *values* reflected in achievement goal constructs (that have been consistently demonstrated to play a significant role in shaping motivational and psychological well-being) might also be reflected in macro-level policy structures that supersede individuals and classrooms.

In Chapter 1, I discussed and reviewed the proliferation of high stakes testing policies in contemporary education. As a final word on the issue, I noted Nichols and Berliner's (2008) eloquent summary of the views of many contemporary academics about high stakes testing policies. I make no apologies for reiterating it as a starting point for this discussion:

> High-stakes testing seems to help with preparing us for the vicissitudes of a competitive world economy, and so it is easily embraced. The needs of the emerging gerontocracy and those who already have some status in society are served by high-stakes testing ... We oppose it for the same reason we are against forcing everyone to participate in extreme sports. If any person

voluntarily chooses to jump the Grand Canyon on a motorcycle, scale Everest, or BASE jump, we wish them luck. We just don't think everyone should be required to engage in the same high stakes sports because, if everyone did, lots of people would be hurt . . . not all of us should be forced to take and fail such exams. In the current high-stakes environment, teachers, students, parents, and American education are being hurt by required high-stakes testing. This policy is corrupting our education system and needs to be stopped. (p. 676)

The idea that goals might operate at individual, classroom *and* on a broader policy level is both morally and politically significant, yet conceptually and theoretically complex. It is morally and politically significant in the sense that goal theory might be able to contribute to Nichols and Berliner's (2007, 2008) fears about the ways in which individuals (e.g. teachers, students and parents) might be 'hurt' in the context of high stakes testing policies. That is, goal theory can provide us with a 'language' (a theoretical and logical narrative) that helps explain how and why individuals are psychologically compromised and affected in the context of high stakes testing. However, consideration of this issue simultaneously adds complexity to the ways in which goal theory's questions, constructs and assumptions might be thought about, and opens up new questions that both extend existing lines of thinking and promise new ones. In what follows, I offer potential avenues for discussion.

Is high stakes testing a policy-level focus on performance goals (and is that good)?

If one attempts to think about policy within goal theory's frame of reference, it would be important to gauge where particular policies appear to be situated in accordance with the conceptual constructs and empirical findings of the theory. In the language of achievement goal theory, it seems difficult to contest that the proliferation of high stakes testing inherently reflects educational policy that is skewed towards prioritising broadly performance-oriented values. In the United States, Marchant (2004) has suggested that high stakes tests are typically national or state-wide standardised achievement tests. Specifically, '. . . how well an individual does on the test is based on a comparison to a large group of test takers . . . "Good" is relative to others at the same grade level' (Marchant, 2004, p. 2) and 'high stakes decisions tend to involve either relative comparisons or reaching a pre-defined cut-off point . . . almost always the decision as to where the cut-off point will be is informed by norm-referenced information' (p. 3).

It is difficult to contest that such policy structures are well positioned to compel students and teachers to focus upon the demonstration of normative adequacy as the primary indicator of educational and academic worth, enticing them into believing that such a focus is a predominant *purpose* of their educational life. Furthermore, it is difficult to see how such forms of high stakes testing are aligned in any way with the belief that academic worth is reflected in personal growth and mastery, or that educational achievement might be simply 'learning for the sake of learning'. Accordingly, high stakes testing seems to reflect a policy-level structure that emphasises and is ultimately positioned around performance-oriented values.

Can we provide evidence to support a major educational policy movement that appears to be rooted in performance-oriented values and beliefs? From a goal theory perspective, is such a policy movement a necessary cornerstone of the education system and is it in the best interests of pupils and teachers? Entering this debate is challenging because (even if we *accepted* the above contention that the policy movement seems to prioritise performance-oriented values) conceptual cloudiness in the recent literature seems to make it difficult to assess goal theory's position with clarity. For example, there have been ambiguous issues at the individual, personal level of goal endorsement, which have led to debate about whether an emphasis on performance-oriented values is detrimental or (potentially) beneficial.

While it has been suggested (Pintrich, 2000) that there is a generally less adaptive set of consequences associated with focusing upon performance goals at the individual and classroom level, there has been some controversy and inconsistency surrounding this assumption. As noted earlier, much of the controversy revolves around empirical data suggesting that *performance-avoidance goals* are consistently linked to maladaptive outcomes and patterns of learning (Carr, 2006; Elliot and Harackiewicz, 1996; Middleton and Midgley, 1997; Skaalvik, 1997) but that *performance-approach* goals have provided less consistent results. Specifically, in relation to performance-approach goals, some (Harackiewicz, Elliot and colleagues) researchers have highlighted their potentially *adaptive* nature and have questioned the logic in making blanket statements that label them as 'generally maladaptive'. For example, a number of studies have identified a positive correlation (although it should be noted that there have equally been numerous studies *failing* to identify any such association) between performance-approach goals and achievement-related outcomes such as test scores, course grades and academic self-efficacy (Bouffard et al., 1995; Elliot and McGregor, 1999; Harackiewicz et al., 1997; Harackiewicz et al., 2000; Midgley and Urdan, 1995; Skaalvik, 1997). Additionally, as Midgley et al. (2001) have pointed out, scattered around the literature are also numerous studies that have identified positive associations between performance-approach goals and outcomes such as self-concept, affect, valuing academic work and exerted effort (Elliot and McGregor, 1999; Elliot et al., 1999; Nicholls et al., 1985; Pajares et al., 2000). Again, however, there are also numerous studies that have failed to identify any such association (or have identified a negative correlation) between performance goals and these outcomes. Adding further to the controversy, there have also been studies suggesting that performance-approach goals have no apparent undermining effects on intrinsic motivation (Elliot and Harackiewicz, 1996; Harackiewicz et al., 2000), whereas other studies (Rawsthorne and Elliot, 1999) have suggested that there is enough evidence to suggest that such goals have a generally deleterious effect on intrinsic motivation, especially when compared to mastery goals.

From a mastery goal perspective, it would seem unwise to prioritise a policy movement that (even) risked encouraging a predominantly performance-oriented focus for a number of reasons. First, Midgley *et al.* (2001) offer a convincing argument to suggest that the current equivocal nature of the findings in relation to performance-approach goals at individual level suggests *only* that such goals can *sometimes* (e.g. if mastery goals are also salient) have *some* positive effects (e.g. a positive relationship with *certain* outcomes such as effort and attainment) for *some* students (e.g. those with high levels of perceived competence). Furthermore, despite these *potential* benefits and *unlike* mastery goals, there are consistent *costs* and *risks* (see Midgley *et al.*, 2001 for a detailed discussion) to a focus on performance-approach goals (e.g. with failure experiences they can evolve into performance-avoidance goals, they are consistently associated with avoidance behaviours, self-handicapping strategies and superficial learning strategies). In their consideration of the performance goal controversy, Midgley *et al.* (2001, p. 83) concluded:

> Is there evidence of the need to adopt a revised goal theory perspective? We do not think so . . . We do not believe there is justification to say that both mastery and performance goals are good . . . performance goals may be adaptive for certain students in certain circumstances as long as mastery goals are also high. This should not be interpreted as proof that it is facilitative for students to be oriented primarily to demonstrating their ability or facilitative for schools to emphasize relative ability and competition among students without emphasizing mastery goals.

Considering the performance goal controversy in the context of the high stakes testing debate, perhaps there is little evidence to defend the proliferation of high stakes testing as a cornerstone of educational policy on the grounds that a fixation upon the demonstration of normative adequacy has been shown to be adaptive under *certain* conditions, for *certain* individuals and in relation to *certain* outcomes. This would seem ill-thought-out justification for placing a policy clearly reflective of performance-oriented values at the core of the education system, not least because educational *equality* (in a motivational sense) is not best encouraged by emphasising values and beliefs that *might* benefit *some* of the people *some* of the time and also brings risks of significant costs to key aspects of learning and motivation (Nicholls and Burton, 1982).

A policy shift towards mastery-oriented values? Process over position

Couldn't policies such as high stakes testing emphasise mastery-oriented values? In the UK, there has certainly been lively debate among policymakers around how best to utilise high stakes testing. Such debate has been contained within a narrow spectrum (i.e. limited to questioning how *best* to evaluate children, teachers and schools [in relation to their 'process' or 'position'?] and how *best* to utilise the results of such evaluations, as opposed to questioning the value in the evaluation exercise per se). For example, the National Association of Head Teachers (NAHT) in the UK argued that they '. . . do not take issue with the *principle* of testing, but with the emphasis on published performance tables and the links between test results and inspection outcomes'. This viewpoint suggested that the problem is not testing children per se but simply *how* the results and data generated are utilised. Based upon this argument, Allen (2012) has pointed out that, in the UK, there has been a shift (in response to strong criticism of a myopic focus upon normative use of high stakes testing) away from an overt, overriding emphasis on such testing, towards an increased emphasis upon mastery- and process-oriented approaches (Weeden et al., 2002) designed to close the gap between actual and desired levels of individual performance (Wiliam and Black, 1996). The rhetoric around such a shift was based upon arguments such as the following:

> Where the classroom culture focuses on rewards, 'gold-stars', grades or place-in-the-class ranking, then pupils look for the ways to obtain the best marks rather than at the needs of their learning . . . .This also generates a 'fear of failure' and leads to efforts by pupils to 'try to build up their self-esteem in other ways'. What is needed is a culture of success, backed by the belief that all can achieve. (Black and Wiliam 1998, pp. 8–9)

At the heart of this UK shift in perspective has been a focus on the process-oriented notion of 'value added', which is conceptualised as the difference between a statistically predicted (an 'expected' sequence of development) performance and actual performance (e.g. a child's score of 'zero' denotes no difference between her actual and predicted performance [i.e. she exhibits the 'expected' level of progress], whereas a score above zero indicates above average progress). Within this system, a 10-level model was conceptualised in the UK whereby (for example) an 'average 8-year-old pupil' ('average' defined according to an assumed sequence of progression calculated by the *Task Group on Assessment and Testing*) would be performing at the lower end of level 3; an average 10-year-old would have achieved level 3; an average 12-year-old level 4 and an average 14-year-old level 5. Based upon statistical analyses of the progressions of populations of actual children, a 'likely-future' is predicted for each child *in relation to* his or her starting score. Similar to the United States (Anderman et al., 2010), these value-added models have used two predominant approaches for calculating likely growth trajectories: (a) a regression line charting the 'average growth' of developmentally similar pupils is used as a template by which judgments of individuals' performance can be facilitated or (b) growth trajectories are calculated for students demonstrating similar achievement at a given starting point (a reference group) and pupils can be judged according to whether they have made similar longitudinal progress to the reference group at a second point in time. Schools can be held accountable by parents and government (and teachers held accountable by school administrators) according to whether or not they achieve the likely-futures calculated for their pupils. Furthermore, those teachers and schools that are able to enhance individual development (over and above what may be predicted by normalised progression routes) would have generated 'value added'.

These shifts are symbolic of a move (that seems to have been mirrored in the United States; Anderman et al., 2010) towards demonstrating the value of 'process over position', transforming children into:

> 'mastery children,' who are motivated by the desire to learn; will tackle difficult tasks in flexible and reflective ways; are confident of success, believing that they can do it if they try. Mastery children 'believe that you can improve your intelligence'. (Allen, 2012, p. 657)

This particular example helps to illustrate how links between goal theory and policy in relation to high stakes testing are likely to be more complex than a simple contention that such tests are a policy-level representation of performance-oriented values. For example, the above shift in the use of test results might be deemed to reflect a more mastery-oriented focus, where schools, teachers, parents and pupils are encouraged to value and judge themselves according to individual progress along an expected trajectory. In the goal theory literature, Anderman et al. (2010) have acknowledged that this approach 'still is not entirely devoid of social comparison' (p. 130) but have suggested that it 'meets the recommendations of goal theorists that all students have the opportunity to be recognized for academic progress and learning' (p. 130). In essence, from a goal theory perspective, it *could* be suggested that such approaches are a positive development.

Viewing the process-oriented shift with suspicion

In the critical psychology literature, Prilleltensky (2008, p. 117) has suggested that 'power suffuses our very own actions as psychologists'. Our own power is all too often masked by a veil of value neutrality that emanates from broader discourses around science and truth frequently distanced from morality. For Prilleltensky (2008), this (a) has simply served to foster a sense of complacency among psychologists about the ways in which their knowledge has been (and could be) translated into policy and discourse (in ways that have frequently been oppressive; see Prilleltensky, 2008, for examples) and (b) has led to what might be viewed as an 'unwitting collusion', where psychologists have obliviously become the agents of the powerful. Perhaps we are more intimately connected to power than we imagine and it is essential that we are critical of (and challenge) the ways in which our knowledge is woven into the narrative of oppressive educational policy.

Foucault's account of neoliberal governmentality (Foucault, 1996; Rose, 1999) highlights the importance of various rational programmes and techniques that try to 'conduct the conduct' of individual behavior in order to obtain specific ends (Rose, 1999). Ong (1999) argued that a key feature of neoliberal governmentality is the way that institutions that are not explicitly political (such as science and education) help shape and sculpt people into particular sorts of economic subjects who are consistent with the aims and objectives of particular strategies of accumulation. According to Foucault (2008, p. 223), this means that neoliberal politics is very much about 'the strategic programming of individuals' activity'. As Barnett (2010) has highlighted, this 'conduct of conduct' increasingly occurs in domains that are not immediately thought of as political, and education has been one such domain. For many critics (Hursh, 2007), high stakes testing has been less about improving student learning and equality than it has about programming individuals to become knowledge workers.

However, as Allen (2012) has noted, sometimes there is a need to tinker with the ways in which 'conduct is conducted' because it becomes clear that there may be more 'effective' ways of shaping and sculpting individuals. By 'effective', I am referring to ways of managing and controlling individuals that might see them transformed into more willing, compliant and industrious followers of dominant prescriptions. For Prilleltensky (2008), this is precisely where psychological knowledge has been a useful ally of the powerful. Put differently, as a credible, legitimate and respectable knowledge base that has frequently sought to calibrate, predict, manage and control individual behaviour (often without much of a mind for the political consequences of such knowledge), it has been suggested that psychology has often colluded with oppressive structural forces.

Connectedly, Allen (2012) has viewed the mastery- or process-oriented shift in UK high stakes testing policy (described above) in the contexts of Foucauldian thought. Her argument suggests that, at first glance, one might applaud a political shift towards lower-stakes mastery-oriented approaches to testing, because they seem more aligned with what motivational theorists might consider to be an 'adaptive' approach to learning for individuals. However, in the context of Foucault's ideas, on a deeper level, such policy shifts have not been viewed as an authentic change in the overriding orientation of such policy. Rather, they have been viewed with suspicion, as a better disguised attempt to transmit the very same educational goals to students under a more 'motivationally acceptable' guise. For Allen (2012), such a policy shift may *suggest* a more pedagogically effective and empowering transformation but the subtext is that underneath, the same ideals prevail:

> What retreats is simply the goad of ranking. In its place pupils learn how to enhance process and develop themselves in apparent harmony with one other, each of them involved in personal formative cycles, occupied in unison within individual feedback-action loops. They learn to become industrious self-enhancers, accepting and implementing external goals. Competition is humanised and disguised and perhaps thereby intensified by this formative technology. (p. 658)

I am not implying that there is necessarily ill intent in the policy shifts described above. However, it is important for motivational psychologists to think carefully about their position in relation to ideas such as the 'conduct of conduct'. Those of us, like Nichols and Berliner (2008), who view high stakes testing as a policy that has ultimately been introduced to prepare 'knowledge workers' and serve the needs of an established gerontocracy ought to carefully question the extent to which our own theories really challenge, resist or facilitate it. In relation to the above, as Allen (2012) argues, simply transforming the *way in which we go about* producing individuals into the same educational product (moving from a 'harsher' performance-oriented normative 'ranking system' to a 'softer' mastery-oriented process of 'individual trajectories') may in the end simply be a smokescreen for disciplinary power seeking to find more acceptable ways of achieving the same instrumental end.

Is the focus on 'individual trajectories' *really* encouraging 'mastery goals'? And what *are* mastery goals anyway?

How do 'mastery goals' feature in the high stakes testing policy shift outlined above? Why do they feature in this way? And how does this fit the ways in which goal theorists think they *should* be conceptualised and utilised? As Anderman et al. (2010) noted, shifting the focus of high stakes testing away from normative ranking systems to individual trajectories certainly seems like a move in the right direction. That is, it seems to be more in line with facilitating a mastery-oriented focus for both teachers and pupils. However, goal theorists should also carefully scrutinise the extent to which they endorse such mastery-oriented shifts in high stakes testing policy. On one level, we must be certain that this type of 'mastery-oriented' focus is *really* something that we believe offers motivational benefits.

Mastery goals have been defined in various ways in the literature and some researchers have argued against the usefulness of a narrow conceptualisation of mastery that limits the construct to whether or not students are focused upon 'getting better' in relation to particular knowledge or skills (Benita et al., 2014; Flum and Kaplan, 2006). For example, Benita et al. (2014) recently highlighted that the contemporary literature on goals has tended to adopt a definition of achievement goals that is biased towards the *aim* of a behaviour (i.e. *what* one is trying to obtain) as opposed to the *reason* for the behaviour (i.e. *why* one is trying to obtain it). They noted that Dweck's (1996) overview of achievement goals specifically focused upon *what* individuals are trying to accomplish (e.g. mastery or normative superiority), without any concern for *why* they try to accomplish it. Similarly, they noted how Elliot's (Elliot, 1999; Elliot and Muruyama, 2008) work has also narrowed the definition of the goal construct so that it is solely limited to *aims-based* criteria. In relation to the mastery goal construct, this has tended to mean that it has been limited to whether one is trying to obtain (a) an absolute standard of competence, such as mastering a specific task, or (b) an intrapersonal standard, such as improving one's competence relative to past performances. This definition of mastery goals has tended to ignore the reasons *why* individuals might be focused upon such aims and has served to facilitate a gradual shift towards empirical work and methodology that has started to view mastery goals solely in terms of *aims* as opposed to *reasons* (Benita *et al.*, 2014).

The problem with restricting the mastery goal construct to an aims-based definition is that it does not take into account the reasons *why* individuals may be focusing upon intrapersonal or absolute standards. It is possible, for example, to focus upon self-improvement because of a sense of external pressure to do so *or* out of a genuine sense of interest and personal autonomy. Furthermore, the reasons why individuals are pursuing such goals may be a significant factor in relation to their motivational benefits. As Benita *et al.* (2014) have suggested:

> Most important, we propose that the advantage of mastery goals in achievement settings is no longer obvious because the benefits of the goal may be strongly related to the type of motivation accompanying it. For example, motives can stem from either personal choice or external control. These two types of motives may predict different emotional and perhaps also performance outcomes for people working toward any goal . . . Hence, people who are trying to do better than they did before (i.e. the aim of improving) may do so with concurrent rigidity and out of a sense of external or internal compulsion (Assor *et al.*, 2004), or they may do so with a sense of choice and interest (Roth *et al.*, 2009).

Providing initial support for their arguments, Benita *et al.* (2014) identified that aims-based mastery goals were more likely to result in positive emotions, interest and enjoyment for students when they were pursuing such goals out of a genuine sense of free, autonomous choice, than when they felt pressured to do so (as though they were 'pawns' pursuing a personally irrelevant end – but in a mastery-oriented fashion). Hence, a focus on intrapersonal standards, in itself, is unlikely to be motivationally beneficial *if* one feels that the aim is imposed or forced.

Researchers have often raised the argument that mastery goals should encompass more than a myopic focus on absolute or intrapersonal standards. Flum and Kaplan (2006) argued for a definition of mastery goals based around personal growth, identity development and exploration (Kaplan and Maehr, 2002):

> Among school children, mastery goals orientation is indicative of students' theories of education that include beliefs that to learn, master matters of substance, and grow as a person, one should invest effort, explore the material, collaborate, approach challenges, take risks, learn from mistakes, be imaginative, and express personal feelings and values.

They argued that a mastery goal construct that includes exploration, expression of personal feelings and personal growth is justified on the grounds that it is these broader elements of 'mastery' that are more likely to foster optimal patterns of development and learning (Flum and Kaplan, 2006). This definition of mastery goals supports Benita *et al.*'s (2014) arguments in the sense that it incorporates the aims to learn and develop *but* with the caveat that these aims should align with or emanate from individuals' broader values, identity and feelings.

Further research is clearly needed. If the motivational benefits associated with mastery goals are linked to the extent to which such goals are perceived to be personally relevant, non-imposed and aligned with personal growth, values and identity, then there are significant implications for the process-oriented high stakes testing policy outlined above. For one thing, it would not be enough to assume that simply imposing the same *aims* upon individuals (i.e. the need to satisfy externally derived standards according to a narrow spectrum of skills and abilities) under a different *guise* (i.e. moving from normative use of test results to a focus upon individual trajectories) would be more likely to result in positive motivational outcomes. Rather, we would also recommend policymakers pay very careful attention to whether pupils genuinely feel that the aims originate from *them*, align with what matters in relation to their *chosen* pathways of growth and identity and do not make them feel like a pawn subjected to the play of external forces. Noam Chomsky (1998, p.43) argued:

> The smart way to keep people passive and obedient is to strictly limit the spectrum of acceptable opinion, but allow very lively debate within that spectrum ... That gives people the sense that there's free thinking going on, while all the time the presuppositions of the system are being reinforced by the limits put on the range of the debate.

For motivational researchers, perhaps restricting the debate around high stakes testing to *how* we might motivate pupils to pursue externally imposed aims is less important than focusing upon *whether* they should be forced to pursue them. Avenues of research such as those offered by Benita *et al.* (2014) may be particularly useful in relation to goal theory's contribution to such lines of thinking because they encourage us to consider (rather than look past) the reasons *why* pupils are pursuing specific aims.

Implications for multiple goals

Rogers (2012) has suggested that there is a significant need to better understand how constructs related to goal theory play out and evolve in the context of real educational life. That is, how are our constructs transformed by the messiness of the everyday life of people caught up in contemporary educational policy? In relation to this, a policy-level focus on high stakes testing that focuses upon value-added, individual trajectories raises interesting possibilities about how individuals and teachers (as agents of classroom goals) might pursue mastery-oriented aims on a *multiple goal* level.

Elliot and Church (1997) conceptualised goals as 'servants' of higher order constructs (i.e. of the needs to achieve and avoid failure). Their model outlined how goal constructs (such as mastery aims) 'serve' particular higher order ends.

For example, as the servant of the higher order needs to avoid failure, a focus on mastery is manifested in mastery avoidance goals. Under this manifestation, research suggests (Sideridis, 2008; Van Yperen *et al.*, 2009) that the motivational benefits associated with such mastery goals are weaker then when they are recruited to serve the higher order need to achieve (i.e. mastery approach goals). If higher order constructs on an *intra*-individual level have been conceptualised to 'recruit' goals as 'servants', then, in a similar vein, it may be worth contemplating *to what end* mastery and performance aims are recruited when they are central features of policy movements (and whether recruiting them for such ends is motivationally adaptive).

In the examples of high stakes testing policy discussed above, what is clear is that the mastery- and performance-related values central to goal theory are not *embodied* in policy as neatly or cleanly as they have been *conceptualised* in academic literature. Rather, they are messy, complicated amalgamations of our constructs 'in practice'. In the example above, the orientation towards individual progress in relation to test data and level attainment is a messy representation of mastery aims in the sense that it reflects (a) a clear focus on the pursuit of progress and mastery (at least if it is narrowly defined as simply getting better in relation to metric indicators) in relation to (b) an individual trajectory that has been (c) *imposed* upon individuals based upon (d) a *normative* idea of what progress is developmentally appropriate for them in relation to (e) narrowly defined outcomes that have been decided for children *a priori* (i.e. are you improving at the rate we think you ought to be improving, in relation to the outcomes and attributes we value?). The very notion of 'mastery' in this real-world example is loaded with complexity and begs consideration of how our constructs are reflected in the context of real world policy-level aims. How mastery aims are woven into the overall narrative of such high stakes testing policy is interesting; individualised progress and trajectories seem to reflect a focus on individual mastery *but* as a vehicle *through which* ultimately normative standards can be satisfied.

In relation to this, recent research into individual-level multiple goals (Carr, 2012; Urdan and Mestas, 2006) has stressed the importance of considering not only which goals are endorsed but also why they are endorsed in relation to *other* goals. As an example, Carr's (2012) recent qualitative examination of individuals endorsing high levels of both mastery *and* performance goals revealed interesting differences in relation to the ways in which certain individuals (who statistically reflected a homogenous subgroup, endorsing high levels of both mastery *and* performance goals) appeared to value and pursue multiple goals. In-depth interviews were able to access subtle, yet significant information about individuals' multiple goal endorsement. For example, a subset of individuals revealed that, while they did gain a sense of achievement and feelings of competence from personal progression and improvement, the *meaning* of such mastery goals was heavily linked to their value in relation to seemingly super-ordinate performance goals. As Carr (2012) summarised, 'the students provided qualitative statements that strongly suggested that they "felt successful" as a function of working hard or showing clear personal improvement because they ultimately perceived such experiences to assist them in demonstrating their superior ability' (pp. 550–551). An extract from one of the interviews in Carr's (2012) study illustrates this point nicely:

Maria: . . . normally my goals are pretty performance based like beating such and such a player or reaching the semi-finals in such and such a tournament. But with, like, 'personal improvements' and 'working hard' no-one can really see that and it doesn't go down on school results pages . . . so I think that's why I don't value that so much.
Interviewer: So why do you agree that they [points to items 'clear personal improvement' and 'working hard'] make you feel successful?
Maria: Because I know that the outcome of it will be me beating people.
Interviewer: And what if that *wasn't* the outcome of trying hard or personal improvement?
Maria: Then I wouldn't feel successful from it.

Hence, for some of these students, mastery goals (defined in this investigation as focusing upon and gaining a sense of competence and satisfaction from personal improvement, progression and learning) were strongly endorsed in the learning context under investigation but were only given *value* in the sense that they served or 'fed into' super-ordinate performance goals.

In relation to this, Senko *et al.* (2011) discussed the challenges that face multiple goal research, noting:

> the multiple goal perspective assumes that students can pursue both mastery and normative goals in some educational settings, and also reap the benefits of each goal. But is it feasible and easy to pursue both goals successfully? Or does pursuing one goal hinder the successful pursuit of the other goal? This thorny issue has received scant attention in goal theory. (p. 36)

Linking this to the above discussions around policy raises questions about how a policy-level atmosphere might create discourse that shapes the ways in which goals are pursued *in relation to each other*. For example, it may be important to explore how policies, such as the move towards individual trajectories in high stakes testing (designed to guide individuals towards normative ends), alter the ways in which mastery goals operate *in relation* to performance goals. It is not inconceivable that in the context of an education system where such central policies set the tone, teachers and individuals might come to appreciate mastery aims *in relation* to their capacity to facilitate achievement of normative (or indeed other types of goal). It will be important for researchers to evaluate (a) the extent to which such hypotheses are plausible in the context of our current education system, and (if they are) (b) the extent to which such deployment of mastery goals (e.g. mastery *as a means to* prescribed normative or performative ends) alters the motivational benefits associated with them. There has been some evidence (Darnon *et al.*, 2009) that students can pursue mastery goals for different reasons (e.g. to please teachers or out of a genuine desire for mastery) and that the motivational effects of mastery goals can be significantly different depending upon the underlying reasons for pursuing them.

Sideridis (2008) and Elliot and McGregor (2001) have provided evidence to suggest that certain manifestations of mastery goals (e.g. mastery avoidance in these studies) are associated with fear of failure, worry, anxiety and negative cognition and emotionality. Sideridis (2008) suggested that although a focus on mastery is generally thought of as an adaptive orientation to achievement, it is likely that there are ways in which this focus might manifest in the real world that are actually harmful and deleterious to affect, motivation and achievement. Policy contexts and initiatives are real-world sites in which to situate research efforts designed to gain an appreciation of the sorts of real-world manifestations of mastery goals that operate. It is an important challenge for goal theorists to ensure that educational policy and practice does not adopt a hollowed out, 'motivationally-benign' version of mastery-oriented aims and we have the opportunity to develop an empirical base from which to do so. This further underscores calls to refine theory around the idea that reasons for goal pursuit might shape the effects of goals on significant outcome variables (Benita *et al.*, 2014; Senko *et al.*, 2011).

Introducing performativity goals

Carr (2015) has critiqued the language of (corporate) 'excellence' that increasingly pervades educational contexts. He noted that 'excellence, it seems, can be clearly defined, quantified, monitored and managed. It has become a narrowly defined "standard of performance" that schools, universities, teachers, lecturers, and students are pressured to strive for. Under the scrutinising gaze of "excellence" all people come to know about themselves is the extent to which they deviate from its image' (excellence is not the only point of education). In essence, this definition of excellence is a direct consequence of a culture of performativity and accountability where students and teachers are 'told' what excellence 'means', must strive to achieve it and are 'judged' accordingly. Writing about performativity, Ball (2003, p. 211) has nicely articulated this point:

> The performances (of individual subjects or organizations) serve as measures of productivity or output, or displays of 'quality', or 'moments' of promotion or inspection. As such they stand for, encapsulate or represent the worth, quality or value of an individual or organization within a narrow field of judgement.

Another way of exploring this pervasive new feature of the educational landscape is to explore how it might be constructing *new* ways of defining what it means for pupils, teachers and schools to 'achieve'. Very recent developments in the goal theory literature have contended that the increasing culture of performativity that permeates educational life has brought about a shift in the way students and teachers define achievement that moves us away from the traditional focus on mastery and performance goals (Cattermole, 2012; Rogers, 2012).

Rogers (2012) has argued for the recognition of a new 'performativity motivation', where students define achievement solely in terms of the performance standards they are required (or require themselves) to 'display' and to which they are held accountable. 'Performativity goals' therefore reflect a sole focus on producing a specific standard of performance, a focus that is devoid of any concern for either normative comparison (which sets them aside from performance goals) or learning and mastery (which distinguishes them from mastery goals). Cattermole (2012, p. 8) suggested:

> Today's high stakes testing rewards educational institutions on the basis of improved or superior performance, and punishes them on the basis of poor or decreasing performance . . . judged on the easily-measured basis of student grades. This means that learning becomes judged on measurable performance such as grades rather than on effective learning strategies. This can easily be communicated to students via teachers who feel pressured to ensure their students get the best possible grades . . . including teaching students how to demonstrate particular grade criteria in their work. Additionally, the aggrandisation of achievement in the UK can result in achievement (measured by grades) becoming an important part of a student's identity and vital to their self-worth. These factors make it likely that students are developing goals that focus on demonstrating competence by achieving particular grades.

In Cattermole's (2012) study, Martin, an A-level student, discusses his focus on such 'performativity goals':

> I was just focusing on grades, I'd just go do the specification and I'd do papers and I'd just go focus on everything to do to do that exam right. Whereas if I was more interested in learning, you know, maybe I wouldn't try as hard with like reading the specification, but I'd go out and read like books that aren't on the specification just for interest, and stuff like reading around the subject, learning more about it.

Cattermole's (2012) work has provided initial qualitative and quantitative support for the usefulness of exploring a specific 'performative goal' construct. She has also demonstrated that the construct seems to be conceptually distinct from mastery and performance goals.

To date there has been little empirical data to explore the motivational significance of 'performativity goals'. However, Rogers's (2012) and Cattermole's (2012) initial work has suggested that they seem to be conceptually distinct variations of achievement goal constructs that students seem increasingly prone to endorsing. Given the pervasive nature of the performativity culture in contemporary education, it would be unsurprising if the ways in which individuals defined achievement and their subsequent aims reflected this. Rogers (2012) has suggested that there will be interesting issues to explore. For example, he has discussed the transition many students make, out of a school system where performativity according to a myopic set of grade descriptors (such as A-levels in the UK) is the norm, to a university system where such grade description is less available and independent learning is (arguably) encouraged. For Rogers (2012), if students are prone to endorsing performativity goals when they enter university then they may find the university environment anxiety provoking and unsuited to the achievement goals they develop as part of their motivational arsenal in school. There will be a need to closely examine (a) the motivational consequences of performativity goals, (b) whether and how such goals operate on a multiple goal level (i.e. do they dampen or impede a focus on mastery and performance goals) and (c) whether and how teachers, schools and universities foster the development of performativity goals or manage them in students. Rogers (2012) has suggested that this important area for future research would serve to position goal theory more squarely within the debate surrounding performative cultures in contemporary education:

> more consideration needs to be given to the meaning of attainment in specific educational contexts before goals can be properly understood. The literature produced to date has often abstracted the assessment context to the point where there may be little transfer to educational situations. If goals are indeed seen to help determine the definition of success then those goals will need to be far more clearly placed within identifiable cultural contexts, bound by both time and place. (p. 31)

Implications for teachers and classroom goals

Researchers (Biddle, 2001; Carr and Weigand, 2008; Duda, 2001; Linnenbrink and Pintrich, 2001; Linnenbrink, 2005) have already entertained the consequences of congruence between individuals' *personal* achievement goals and goals emphasised in the *classroom*. As discussed earlier, Linnenbrink and Pintrich (2001) discussed the idea of (a) a *buffering hypothesis* (where a *personal* mastery orientation will buffer the negative effects of *classroom* performance goals *or* classroom mastery goals will buffer the negative effects of personal performance goals) and (b) a *matching hypothesis* (where classroom contexts that are congruent with students' personal goals are most beneficial as they support personal goal pursuits).

Exploring this, Carr and Weigand's (2008) data suggested that personal endorsement of high mastery/high performance (-approach) goals protected motivational responses (i.e. self-determined motivation and positive affect) across mastery *and* performance classroom environments. Whereas all other personal goal profile groups (high mastery/low performance, low mastery/high performance, low mastery/low performance) experienced dampened motivational responses in the context of a performance-oriented classroom. The authors suggested that this seemed to provide evidence in support of both a buffering *and* a matching hypothesis. That is, high mastery/high performance oriented pupils had an advantage over high mastery/low performance pupils because they were able to satisfy personal goals in *either* perceived mastery *or* performance class climates (as both emphasised achievement concerns congruent with an aspect of their personal goal profile). In addition to this, high mastery/high performance individuals *also* had strong personal mastery goals to fall back on in situations where normative ability was jeopardised (giving them an advantage over low mastery/high performance individuals). Hence, high mastery/high performance individuals were able to satisfy elements of their achievement goal profile when exposed to either perceived mastery or perceived performance climates, and they also had an element of protection from the potential maladaptive concomitants of performance goals/climates because they also endorsed personal mastery goals. This study did not include classrooms in which multiple goals were emphasised. In relation to this, (and in line with the *selective hypothesis* forwarded by Barron and Harackiewicz, 2001), Linnenbrink (2005) hypothesised that a combined mastery–performance classroom might allow students with mastery goals, performance goals or both to readily pursue personal goals.

In a similar vein, mismatch between goals that are espoused at individual, classroom and wider policy level have the potential to open up interesting avenues for further research. Researchers (Maehr and Anderman, 1993; Maehr and Midgely, 1996) have recognised that changes in goals at the classroom level of representation may be heavily dependent upon broader changes in relation to the school culture within which teachers and their classrooms are nested. Maehr and Anderman (1993) argued that changes in the structural features of classrooms (e.g. in the TARGET structures forwarded by Epstein, 1989) can only be brought about when higher order school cultures themselves are congruent with these values:

> In sum, our argument is that school culture can be changed by changing how the school goes about its business. Implicit within everyday policies, practices, and procedures are basic beliefs about the meaning of teaching and learning. These need to be examined and sometimes changed. (Maehr and Anderman, 1993, p. 599)

Maehr and Anderman (1993) went on to report an innovative school-university collaboration project that sought to transform the school culture of two elementary and two middle schools in the Detroit area. Their project sought to transform school culture by introducing and implementing an array of changes to policy, practice and everyday procedures that influenced goals (e.g. moves towards abolishing ability groupings, broadening the meaning of learning, removing 'honor rolls', moving away from normative grading practices), seeking to emphasise and embrace a mastery-oriented ethos and downplay emphasis on performance-oriented values.

Some of the most interesting aspects of change in school culture that Maehr and Anderman (1993) reported related to a noticeable shift in the general language and discourse teachers employed. Specifically, they noticed a shift in the sense that teachers began (a) to critically evaluate their former practices (i.e. 'competitive' practices that they had often questioned on a motivational level but about which they felt powerless and hopeless in relation to effecting change), (b) to gain a sense of empowerment in relation to their agency in creating an alternative culture and (c) to replace 'blaming and wondering why' (i.e. displacing blame about lack of student motivation onto students themselves or onto 'unchangeable' policy) with genuine engagement with ideas about how they might best motivate and inspire their students. As Maehr and Anderman (1993) themselves suggested, 'in particular, teachers and the staff as a whole have engaged in an increasingly thorough examination of their philosophy of education, their theory of school . . . That is the most painful – but also the most significant – part of what is beginning to occur' (p. 602).

Clearly, teachers are significant agents in the construction of structural representations of achievement goals at the classroom level (Ames, 1992; Nicholls et al., 1989; Paris and Newman, 1990). Maehr and Anderman's (1993) efforts highlight how it is essential to pay attention to the broader social, political and organisational structures within which teachers are themselves situated and that may have a significant bearing on the development of their belief systems about schooling in general, their goals for children's learning and the hope and aspirations they have for creating optimal cultures for teaching, learning and motivation. However, issues related to congruence and mismatching between goal representations emphasised at the various structural levels of representation are likely to be complex.

In the context of the contemporary debate, it is possible to appreciate that teachers valuing (and seeking to emphasise) a genuinely mastery-oriented *classroom* level goal structure may now be (arguably, more than ever) sailing against a strong headwind as they operate on a day to day basis under the requirements of centralised policy that requires them to enact and espouse opposing values. Over twenty years since the school culture transformation efforts of psychologists such as Maehr, Anderman and Midgely (Maehr and Anderman, 1993; Maehr and Midgely, 1996), goal theory has offered little in relation to these potential conflicts, while policy has drifted towards a myopic focus on performativity and normative attainment, holding pupils, teachers and schools accountable for such attainment, and shaping educational practices accordingly. In a paper presented at a recent British Psychological Society seminar at Cambridge University, Remedios and McClellan (2009) argued that what is urgently needed in the goal theory literature is a thorough examination of whether it remains possible for the assumptions espoused by achievement goal theorists to make an educational impact at classroom level when classrooms are, more than ever, superseded by a broader layer of oppositional policy.

Consideration of how a policy-level structural layer of goal representation might interact with and influence classroom and individual level goals to shape the life world of contemporary teachers and pupils holds great potential for future research that integrates and synthesises goal theory with ideas from other domains of educational research. For example, in the sociology of education, there has been attention devoted to the (increasingly apparent) 'inner conflict' that can play out in the lives of many teachers. Ball's work (2003) emphasises how the scrutinising gaze of myopic educational policies (to which they are held accountable) means that the professional lives of teachers increasingly requires them to organise themselves in accordance with the targets, indicators and evaluations to which they are held accountable. As Ball (2003) suggested, for many, it has become part of the job

> ... to set aside personal beliefs and commitments and live an existence of calculation. The new performative worker is a promiscuous self, an enterprising self, with a passion for excellence. For some, this is an opportunity to make a success of themselves, for others it portends inner conflicts, inauthenticity and resistance. It is also suggested that performativity produces opacity rather than transparency as individuals and organizations take ever greater care in the construction and maintenance of fabrications. (p. 215)

Upon such a platform, the professional life of some teachers involves 'enacting' educational policies that reflect values and beliefs completely incongruent with their deeper values and morals. Ball's (2003, p. 216) paper produces the following quotes from teachers caught in this predicament:

> What happened to my creativity? What happened to my professional integrity? What happened to the fun in teaching and learning? What Happened? *(G. E. Johnson)*

> I find myself thinking that the only way I can save my sanity, my health and my relationship with my future husband is to leave the profession. I don't know what else I could do, having wanted to teach all my life, but I feel I am being forced out, forced to choose between a life and teaching. *(Name not supplied)*

> I was a primary school teacher for 22 years but left in 1996 because I was not prepared to sacrifice the children for the glory of politicians and their business plans for education. *(Christopher Draper)*

> It's as though children are mere nuts and bolts on some distant production line, and it angers me to see them treated so clinically in their most sensitive and formative years. *(Roma Oxford)*

In the context of goal theory, there will be important questions to address that clearly relate to such literature. For example, as discussed above, the neoliberal educational platform has firmly established a culture of performativity that has colonised teachers' lives, robbed them of their autonomy and de-professionalised them (Ball, 2003; Jeffrey and Woods, 1998). This phenomenon has fundamentally altered the ways in which teachers and pupils are likely to experience teaching and learning, and goal theory has the potential to contribute significantly to the development of our understanding of this.

For example, in the face of accountability to rigid high stakes testing policies, do teachers feel pressured into focusing upon particular aims that they do not personally endorse (and perhaps even reject) and that are incongruent with their personal goals? In the context of such incongruence, how are individuals affected by the inner conflict between achievement values they are 'required' to endorse and espouse in the classroom and those that more closely align with their moral code? How does policy backdrop create barriers and resistance to the development of classrooms that place genuine mastery orientation at the centre of learning? How can/do teachers, under increasing pressure to become agents of policies such as NCLB, develop spaces where their classrooms are genuinely agents of a child's personal growth and mastery? Lipman's (2004) ethnographic investigation of inner city schools in Chicago demonstrated how teachers' creativity and ingenuity in relation to literacy goals for their pupils (who were predominantly from immigrant families) were frequently undermined by the pressure to teach these pupils according to standardised tests and trajectories. She documented the inner conflict and genuine sadness teachers felt at not being able to help immigrant children develop knowledge and skills that might better equip them to understand *their* world and the development of knowledge and skills that would help them pass the national standardised tests imposed upon them. Such issues are notably absent in the goal theory literature and would reflect a shift towards a more explicit consideration of how the theory might contribute to current policy debates and wider literature outside of the field of educational psychology.

Such issues might prompt researchers to think about how policy-level goal structures might be creating a predicament ripe for *goal conflict* to become part of contemporary teachers' working lives. Bordreaux and Ozer (2012) have discussed the significance of goal conflict for motivational theory and have highlighted that goal conflict can occur when the focus on one goal undermines or distorts the pursuit of other valued goals. They argued that motivational theory has been slow to develop an empirical foundation for the investigation of goal conflict, particularly when it has long been documented in the broader psychological literature (Gray and McNaughton, 2000; Lewin, 1935; Miller, 1944) that such conflict plays a significant role in personality functioning. More specifically, Bordreaux and Ozer (2012) have suggested that the *implications* of goal conflict for health and well-being, behavioural inhibition and general motivational responses remain uncharted territory in need of empirical investigation and theoretical consideration. From the discussion in this paper, it is concerning that policy-level representations of achievement goals might create a platform that pulls individuals into a perpetual state of goal conflict in relation to the classroom goals they feel pressured to emphasise and the personal goals they authentically value as educators. A worthy contemporary challenge for goal theory is to develop a conceptual and empirical knowledge base that contributes to this issue.

Concluding thoughts

Fox *et al.* (2009) have suggested that psychological research can create knowledge in a vacuum or it can ask questions and generate knowledge that has clearly been designed to facilitate movement towards social justice for populations of interest or society at large. As an educator, it is difficult to disagree with Bernstein's (1996, p. 87) contention that 'the principles of the market and its managers are more and more the managers of the policy and practices of education'. As the neoliberal educational landscape increasingly produces policy frameworks based around notions such as high stakes testing and cultures of performativity and accountability, it will be important for educational psychologists to develop and organise their knowledge base with this in mind. This means critically engaging with the ways in which such policy can be oppressive and unjust, illuminating the plight of those who suffer because of it and exploring how theoretical constructs, language and knowledge might challenge questionable assumptions.

In this chapter, I sought to begin the processes of reflection and re-examination that critical psychologists (Fowers, 2015; Louis *et al.*, 2014) have suggested will be particularly important in relation to this. Such reflection and re-examination of our ideas, constructs and assumptions in the context of key features of the neoliberal educational landscape can help us better appreciate how goal theory might create a theoretical space that significantly contributes to such efforts. The discussion in this chapter suggests that there may be particularly important areas of research that have the potential to develop knowledge that helps to better understand the *motivational* and *psychological* consequences of neoliberal educational policy and calls for genuine motivational equality in our education system. The following points summarise some of the key areas discussed:

- Can high stakes testing *ever* be a policy that genuinely serves to motivate teachers and young people and facilitate motivational equality in our education system?
- Are moves towards a process-oriented use of high stakes test results in relation to individual trajectories *really* an example of a more mastery-oriented approach that is likely to stimulate more positive motivational consequences? Is a focus upon individual trajectories *really* motivational if one fails to consider the *reasons why* such intra-individual progress is being pursued? Can it be *genuinely* motivating to pursue what appear to be mastery-oriented aims *if* one is doing so out of a sense of external or internal pressure? Is this type of mastery-oriented focus what we recommend mastery-oriented motivation *should* be?
- In the face of the proliferation of high stakes testing and performativity cultures, how are goals pursued *in relation to each other*? Are learning and mastery goals pursued as an end in themselves? Or are they increasingly the servants of more normative or performative goals that are higher up the pecking order in relation to what matters? How might this affect the motivational consequences of these goals?

- How might the introduction of a construct such as 'performativity goals' better reflect the changing nature of the educational landscape? What are the motivational consequences of such goals? How do they interact with and influence pursuit of traditional types of achievement goals? Are they the motivational manifestation of the new performativity culture and, if so, what does this mean for teachers and young people?
- How do teachers *experience* the conflicts they face between goals they are pressured to espouse by policy and goals that they believe are more meaningful but do not have the opportunity to emphasise in a culture of accountability? How is such conflict experienced, managed and played out in the lives of the new performative teachers?

Ultimately, more closely developing our knowledge around issues such as these may serve to ensure that our knowledge base remains *relevant* to the concerns and struggles that are part and parcel of the neoliberal educational landscape for millions of teachers, children and young people (Patrick *et al.*, 2011). Furthermore, developing our knowledge in these ways might also help to ensure that we develop and maintain a critical consciousness in relation to the political landscape.

As a final note, it is also important to be mindful of the fact that the development of a critical consciousness in our knowledge base simply isn't enough. As Prilleltensky (2008) has noted, time is short and suffering vast in our schools and it is time that we drew direct links between our research and the ways it can be converted into transformative potential and *action*. In relation to this, knowledge is only part of the picture. In their efforts to transform school cultures, one of the most significant lessons Maehr and Anderman (1993) learned was the enormous importance of enabling teachers and learners to critically appraise their practices and develop a sense of empowerment in relation to their agency in creating an alternative culture. It is difficult to believe that almost a quarter of a century has passed since their efforts to genuinely transform school cultures. In relation to the effort to empower, enable and resist oppressive educational policy *with* those who are oppressed *by* it, goal theory has, to date, been surprisingly inactive. It is time to develop a more critical, active and transformative space.

References

Ablard, K. and Parker, W. (1997). Parents' achievement goals and perfectionism in their academically talented children, *Journal of Youth and Adolescence*, 26(6), 651–67.

Allen, A. (2012). Cultivating the myopic learner: The shared project of high-stakes and low-stakes assessment. *British Journal of Sociology of Education*, 33(5), 641–59.

Ames, C. (1984). Competitive, cooperative, and individualistic goal structures: A motivational analysis. In R.E. Ames and C. Ames (eds), *Research on Motivation in Education: Vol. 1. Student motivation* (pp. 177–207). New York: Academic Press.

Ames, C. (1992). Classrooms: Goals, structures, and student motivation. *Journal of Educational Psychology*, 84(3), 261–71.

Ames, C. and Archer, J. (1987). Mothers' beliefs about the role of effort and ability in school learning, *Journal of Educational Psychology*, 79(4), 409–14.

Ames, C. and Archer, J. (1988). Achievement goals in the classroom: Students' learning strategies and motivation processes, *Journal of Educational Psychology*, *80*(3), 260–67.
Anderman, E.M. (2011). Educational psychology in the twenty-first century: Challenges for our community. *Educational Psychologist*, *46*(3), 185–96.
Anderman, E.M., Anderman, L.H., Yough, M.S. and Gimbert, B.G. (2010). Value-added models of assessment: Implications for motivation and accountability. *Educational Psychologist*, *45*(2), 123–37.
Assor, A., Kaplan, H. and Roth, G. (2002). Choice is good, but relevance is excellent: Autonomy-enhancing and suppressing teacher behaviours predicting students' engagement in schoolwork. *British Journal of Educational Psychology*, *72*(2), 261–78.
Assor, A., Roth, G. and Deci, E.L. (2004). The emotional costs of parents' conditional regard: A self-determination theory analysis. *Journal of Personality*, *72*(1), 47–88.
Atkinson, J. (1957). Motivational determinants of risk-taking behavior. *Psychological Review*, *64*(6), 359–72.
Ball, S. (2003). The teacher's soul and the terrors of performativity. *Journal of Educational Policy*, *18*(2), 215–28.
Barnett, C. (2010). Publics and markets: What's wrong with neoliberalism? In S.J. Smith, R. Pain, S.A. Marston and J.P. Jones III (eds), *The Sage Handbook of Social Geography* (pp. 269–96). London: Sage.
Barron, K.E. and Harackiewicz, J.M. (2001). Achievement goals and optimal motivation: Testing multiple goal models. *Journal of Personality and Social Psychology*, *80*(5), 706–22.
Benita, M., Roth, G. and Deci, E.L. (2014). When are mastery goals more adaptive? It depends on experiences of autonomy support and autonomy. *Journal of Educational Psychology*, *106*(1), 258–67.
Bernstein, B. (1996). *Pedagogy Symbolic Control and Identity*. London: Taylor & Francis.
Biddle, S. (2001). Enhancing motivation in physical education. In G. Roberts (ed.), *Advances in Motivation in Sport and Exercise*. Champaign, IL: Human Kinetics.
Black, P. and Wiliam, D. (1998). *Inside the Black Box: Raising Standards Through Classroom Assessment*. London: King's College London School of Education.
Bordreaux, M. and Ozer, D. (2012). Goal conflict, goal striving, and psychological well-being. *Motivation and Emotion*, *37*(3), 433–43.
Bouffard, T., Boisvert, J., Vezeau, C. and Larouche, C. (1995). The impact of goal orientation on self-regulation and performance among college students. *British Journal of Educational Psychology*, *65*(3), 317–29.
Carr, S. (2006). An examination of multiple goals in children's physical education: Motivational effects of goal profiles and the role of perceived climate in multiple goal development. *Journal of Sports Sciences*, *24*(3), 281–97.
Carr, S. (2012). High task/High ego oriented students' reasons for endorsing task and ego goals in the context of physical education. *Applied Psychology: An International Review*, *61*(4), 540–63.
Carr, S. (2015). Excellence is not the only point of education. *The Conversation*, 4 March 2015. Available at https://theconversation.com/excellence-is-not-the-only-point-of-education-38148
Carr, S. and Weigand, D.A. (2001). Parental, peer, teacher, and sporting hero influence on the goal orientations of children in physical education. *European Physical Education Review*, *7*, 305–28.
Carr, S. and Weigand, D.A. (2008). Children's goal profiles and perceptions of the motivational climate: Interactive association with self-determined motivation and affective patterns in physical education. *Journal of Social, Behavioral, and Health Sciences*, *2*, 8–32.

Cattermole, S. (2012). *An exploration of performativity and the changing motivations of advanced level students.* Unpublished Doctoral Thesis, University of Lancaster, UK.

Chomsky, N. (1998). *The Common Good.* Berkeley, CA: Odonian Press.

Covington, M.V. and Omelich, C.L. (1984). Task-oriented versus competitive learning structures: Motivational and performance consequences. *Journal of Educational Psychology*, 76(6), 1038–50.

Darnon, C., Dompnier, B., Delmas, F., Pulfrey, C. and Butera, F. (2009). Achievement goal promotion at university: Social desirability and social utility of mastery and performance goals. *Journal of Personality and Social Psychology*, 96(1), 119–34.

Deci, E. and Ryan, R. (1990). A motivational approach to the self: Integration in Personality. In R. Dienstbier (ed.), *Nebraska Symposium on Motivation* (Vol. 38). Lincoln: University of Nebraska Press.

Duda, J.L. and Hall, H.K. (2001). Achievement goal theory in sport: Recent extensions and future directions. In R. Singer, H. Hausenblas and C. Janelle (eds), *Handbook of Research in Sport Psychology* (2nd edn, pp. 417–34). New York: John Wiley.

Dweck, C.S. (1986). Motivational processes affecting learning. *American Psychologist*, 41(10), 1040–48.

Dweck, C.S. (1996). Capturing the dynamic nature of personality. *Journal of Research in Personality*, 30(3), 348–62.

Dweck, C. and Elliott, E. (1983). Achievement motivation. In E. Heatherington (ed.), *Handbook of Child Psychology* (Vol. 4). New York: Wiley.

Dweck, C.S. and Leggett, E.L. (1988). A social-cognitive approach to motivation and personality. *Psychological Review*, 95(2), 256–73.

Elliot, A.J. (1997). Integrating the "classic" and "contemporary" approaches to achievement motivation: A hierarchical model of approach and avoidance achievement motivation. In M.L. Maehr and P.R. Pintrich (eds), *Advances in Motivation and Achievement* (Vol. 10, pp. 143–79). Greenwich, CT: JAI Press.

Elliot, A.J. (1999). Approach and avoidance motivation and achievement goals. *Educational Psychologist*, 34(3), 169–89.

Elliot, A. (2005). A conceptual history of the achievement goal construct. In A. Elliot and C. Dweck (eds), *Handbook of Competence and Motivation* (pp. 52–72). New York: Guilford Press.

Elliot, A.J. and Harackiewicz, J.M. (1996). Approach and avoidance achievement goals and intrinsic motivation: A mediational analysis. *Journal of Personality and Social Psychology*, 70(3), 461–75.

Elliot, A.J. and Church, M. (1997). A hierarchical model of approach and avoidance achievement motivation. *Journal of Personality and Social Psychology*, 72(1), 218–32.

Elliot, A.J. and McGregor, H.A. (1999). Test anxiety and the hierarchical model of approach and avoidance achievement motivation. *Journal of Personality and Social Psychology*, 76(4), 628–44.

Elliot, A.J., McGregor, H.A. and Gable, S. (1999). Achievement goals, study strategies, and exam performance: A mediational analysis. *Journal of Educational Psychology*, 91(3), 549–63.

Elliot, A.J. and McGregor, H.A. (2001). A 2x2 achievement goal framework. *Journal of Personality and Social Psychology*, 80(3), 501–19.

Elliot, A.J. and Murayama, K. (2008). On the measurement of achievement goals: Critique, illustration, and application. *Journal of Educational Psychology*, 100(3), 613–28.

Elliot, A J. and Dweck, D. (2005). Competence as the core of achievement motivation. In A. Elliot and C. Dweck (eds), *Handbook of Competence and Motivation*. New York: Guilford Press.

Elliott, E.S. and Dweck, C.S. (1988). Goals: An approach to motivation and achievement. *Journal of Personality and Social Psychology*, 54(1), 5–12.

Epstein, J.L. (1988). Effective schools or effective students: Dealing with diversity. In R. Haskins and D. Macrae (eds), *Policies for America's Public Schools: Teachers, Equity, and Indicators* (pp. 89–126). Norwood, NJ: Ablex.

Fox, D., Prilleltensky, I. and Austin, S. (2009). Critical psychology for social justice: Concerns and dilemmas. In D. Fox, I. Prilleltensky and S. Austin (eds), *Critical Psychology: An Introduction* (pp. 3–20). London: Sage.

Flum, H. and Kaplan, A. (2006). Exploratory orientation as an educational goal. *Educational Psychologist*, 41(2), 99–110.

Foucault, M. (1996). *Istoria nebuniei în perioada clasică*. Bucuresti: Humanitas.

Fowers, B.J. (2015). The promise of a flourishing theoretical psychology. *Journal of Theoretical and Philosophical Psychology*, 35(3), 145–59.

Gray, J.A. and McNaughton, N. (2000). *The Neuropsychology of Anxiety: An Enquiry into the Functions of the Septo-Hippocampal System*. Oxford: Oxford University Press.

Harackiewicz, J., Barron, K. and Elliot, A. (1998). Rethinking achievement goals: When are they adaptive for college students and why? *Educational Psychologist*, 33(1), 1–21.

Harackiewicz, J.M., Barron, K.E., Carter, S.M., Lehto, A.T. and Elliot, A.J. (1997). Predictors and consequences of achievement goals in the college classroom: Maintaining interest and making the grade. *Journal of Personality and Social Psychology*, 73(6), 1284–95.

Harackiewicz, J.M., Barron, K.E., Tauer, J.M., Carter, S.M. and Elliot, A.J. (2000). Short-term and long-term consequences of achievement goals: Predicting interest and performance over time. *Journal of Educational Psychology*, 92(2), 316–30.

Hulleman, C.S., Schrager, S.M., Bodmann, S.M. and Harackiewicz, J.M. (2010). A meta-analytic review of achievement goal measures: Different labels for the same constructs or different constructs with similar labels? *Psychological Bulletin*, 136(3), 422–49.

Hursh, D. (2007). 'No child left behind' and the rise of neoliberal education policies. *American Educational Research Journal*, 44(3), 493–518.

Kaplan, A., Gheen, M. and Midgley, C. (2002). Classroom goal structure and students' disruptive behaviour, *British Journal of Educational Psychology*, 72(2), 191–211.

Kaplan, A. and Maehr, M.L. (2002). Adolescents' achievement goals: Situating motivation in sociocultural contexts. *Academic Motivation of Adolescents*, 2, 125–67.

Kaplan, A., Middleton, M., Urdan, T. and Midgley, C. (2002). Achievement goals and goal structures. In C. Midgley (ed.), *Goals, Goal Structures, and Patterns of Adaptive Learning* (pp. 21–53). Mahwah, NJ: Erlbaum.

Lewin, K. (1935). *A dynamic theory of personality: Selected papers*, translated by D.E. Adams and K.E. Zener. New York: McGraw-Hill.

Linnenbrink, E.A. (2004). Person and context: Theoretical and practical concerns in achievement goal theory. In P.R. Pintrich and M.L. Maehr (eds), *Advances in Motivation and Achievement: Motivating Students, Improving Schools: The Legacy of Carol Midgley* (Vol. 13, pp. 159–84). Greenwich, CT: JAI Press.

Linnenbrink, E.A. (2005). The dilemma of performance-approach goals: The use of multiple goal contexts to promote students' motivation and learning. *Journal of Educational Psychology*, 97(2), 197–213.

Linnenbrink, E.A. and Pintrich, P.R. (2001). Multiple goals, multiple contexts: The dynamic interplay between personal goals and contextual goal stresses. In S. Volet and S. Jarvela (eds), *Motivation in Learning Contexts: Theoretical and Methodological Implications* (pp. 251–69). Amsterdam: Pergamon Press.

Lipman, P. (2004). *High-Stakes Education: Inequality, Globalization and Urban School Reform*. New York: Routledge.

Louis, W.R., Mavor, K.I., La Macchia, S.T. and Amiot, C.E. (2014). Social justice and psychology: What is, and what should be. *Journal of Theoretical and Philosophical Psychology*, 34(1), 14–27.

Maehr, M.L. (1989). Thoughts about motivation. In C. Ames and R. Ames (eds), *Research on Motivation in Education* (Vol. 3, pp. 299–315). New York: Academic Press.

Maehr, M.L. and Anderman, E.M. (1993). Reinventing schools for early adolescents: Emphasizing task goals. *Elementary School Journal*, 93(5), 593–610.

Maehr, M. and Midgley, C. (1991). Enhancing student motivation: A schoolwide approach, *Educational Psychologist*, 26(3–4), 399–427.

Maehr, M.L. and Midgley, C. (1996). *Transforming School Cultures*. Boulder, CO: Westview Press.

Maehr, M.L. and Zusho, A. (2009). Achievement goal theory: The past, present, and future. In K. Wentzel and A. Wigfield (eds), *Handbook of Motivation in School* (p. 77–104). New York: Routledge.

Marchant, G.J. (2004). What is at stake with high stakes testing? A discussion of issues and research, *Ohio Journal of Science*, 104(2), 2–7.

McClelland, D.C. (1951). *Personality*. New York: Dryden Press.

Meece, J.L. and Holt, K. (1993). A pattern analysis of students' achievement goals. *Journal of Educational Psychology*, 85(4), 582–90.

Meece, J., Anderman, E.M. and Anderman, L.H. (2006). Structures and goals of educational settings: Classroom goal structure, student motivation, and academic achievement. *Annual Review of Psychology*, 57(1), 487–504.

Middleton, M.J. and Midgley, C. (1997). Avoiding the demonstration of lack of ability: An underexplored aspect of goal theory. *Journal of Educational Psychology*, 89(4), 710–18.

Midgley, C, Arunkumar, R. and Urdan, T. (1996). If I don't do well tomorrow, there's a reason: Predictors of adolescents' use of academic self-handicapping behavior. *Journal of Educational Psychology*, 88(3), 423–34.

Midgley, C. and Urdan, T. (1995). Predictors of middle school students' use of self-handicapping strategies. *Journal of Early Adolescence*, 15(4), 389–411.

Midgley, C., Kaplan, A. and Middleton, M.J. (2001). Performance-approach goals: Good for what, for whom, under what circumstances, at what cost? *Journal of Educational Psychology*, 93(1), 77–86.

Miller, N.E. (1944). Experimental studies of conflict. In J. Mc. V. Hunt (ed.), *Personality and the Behavior Disorders* (pp. 431–65). New York: Ronald Press Company.

Molden, D.C. and Dweck, C.S. (2006). Finding "meaning" in psychology: A lay theories approach to self-regulation, social perception, and social development. *American Psychologist*, 61(3), 192–203.

Morris, R.L. and Kavussanu, M. (2008). Antecedents of approach-avoidance goals in sport. *Journal of Sports Sciences*, 26(5), 465–76.

Murayama, K. and Elliot, A.J. (2009). The joint influence of personal achievement goals and classroom goal structures on achievement-related outcomes. *Journal of Educational Psychology*, 101(2), 432–47.

Nichols, S.L. and Berliner, D.C. (2008). Why has high-stakes testing so easily slipped into contemporary American life? *Phi Delta Kappa*, 89(9), 672–76.

Nichols, S.L. and Berliner, D.C. (2007). *Collateral Damage: How High-Stakes Testing Corrupts America's Schools*. Cambridge, MA: Harvard Education.

Nicholls, J.G. (1984). Achievement motivation: Conceptions of ability, subjective, experience, task choice and performance. *Psychological Review*, 91(3), 328–46.

Nicholls, J.G. (1989). *The Competitive Ethos and Democratic Education*. Cambridge, MA: Harvard University Press.

Nicholls, J.G. and Burton, J.T. (1982). Motivation and equality. *Elementary School Journal*, 82(4), 67–78.

Nicholls, J.G., Patashnick, M. and Nolen, S.B. (1985). Adolescents' theories of education. *Journal of Educational Psychology*, 77(6), 683–92.

Nicholls, J.G., Cheung, P., Lauer, J. and Patashnick, N. (1989). Individual differences in academic motivation: Perceived ability, goals, beliefs, and values. *Learning and Individual Differences, 1*(1), 63–84.

Ong, A. (1999). *Flexible Citizenship. The Cultural Logics of Transnationality*. Durham NC: Duke University Press.

Pajares, F., Britner, S. and Valiante, G. (2000). Relation between achievement goals and self-beliefs of middle school students in writing and science. *Contemporary Educational Psychology, 25*(4), 406–22.

Papaioannou, A.G., Ampatzoglou, G., Kalogiannis, P. and Sagovits, A. (2008). Social agents, achievement goals, satisfaction and academic achievement in youth sport. *Psychology of Sport and Exercise, 9*(2), 122–41.

Parker, I. (2009). Critical Psychology and Revolutionary Marxism. *Theory and Psychology, 19*(1), 71–92.

Paris, S.G. and Newman, R.S. (1990). Developmental aspects of self-regulated learning. *Educational Psychologist, 25*(1), 87–102.

Patrick, H., Anderman, L.H., Bruening, P.S. and Duffin, L.C. (2011). The role of educational psychology in teacher education: Three challenges for educational psychologists. *Educational Psychologist, 46*(2), 71–83.

Pintrich, P.R. and Garcia, T. (1991). Student goal orientation and self-regulation in the college classroom. In M.L. Maehr and P.R. Pintrich (eds), *Advances in Motivation and Achievement* (Vol. 7, pp. 371–402). Greenwich, CT: JAI Press.

Pintrich, P.R. and Schunk, D.H. (2002). *Motivation in Education: Theory, Research, and Practice*. Englewood Cliffs, NJ: Merrill.

Pintrich, P.R. (2000). An achievement goal theory perspective on issues in motivation terminology, theory, and research. *Contemporary Educational Psychology, 25*(1), 92–104.

Pintrich, P.R. and Schunk, D.H. (1996). *Motivation in Education: Theory, Research, and Applications*. Englewood Cliffs, NJ: Prentice Hall Merrill.

Prilleltensky, I. (2008). The role of power in wellness, oppression, and liberation: The promise of psychopolitical validity. *Journal of Community Psychology, 36*(2), 116–36.

Rawsthorne, L.J. and Elliot, A.J. (1999). Achievement goals and intrinsic motivation: A meta-analytic review. *Personality and Social Psychology Review, 3*(4), 326–44.

Remedios, R. and McClellan, R. (2009). Goal theory and self-determination theory: Theory and current debates. *British Psychological Society Science Quarterly, 25*, 226–51. Seminar Series, Cambridge University, UK.

Rogers, C. (2012). Transition, self-regulation, independent learning and goal theory. *Psychology of Education Review, 36*, 26–31.

Rose, N. (1999). *Powers of Freedom: Reframing Political Thought*. Cambridge: Cambridge University Press.

Roth, G., Assor, A., Niemiec, C.P., Ryan, R.M. and Deci, E.L. (2009). The emotional and academic consequences of parental conditional regard: Comparing conditional positive regard, conditional negative regard, and autonomy support as parenting practices. *Developmental Psychology, 45*, 1119–42.

Senko, C., Hulleman, C.S. and Harackiewicz, J.M. (2011). Achievement goal theory at the crossroads: Old controversies, current challenges, and new directions. *Educational Psychologist, 46*(1), 26–47.

Sideridis, G.D. (2008). The regulation of affect, anxiety, and stressful arousal from adopting mastery-avoidance goal orientations. *Stress and Health, 24*(1), 55–69.

Skaalvik, E. (1997). Self-enhancing and self-defeating ego orientation: Relations with task and avoidance orientation, achievement, self-perceptions, and anxiety. *Journal of Educational Psychology, 89*(1), 71–81.

Urdan, T.C. (1997). Achievement goal theory: Past results, future directions. In M.L. Maehr and P.R. Pintrich (eds), *Advances in Motivation and Achievement* (Vol. 10, pp. 99–141). Greenwich, CT: JAI Press.

Urdan, T. and Turner, J. (2005). Competence motivation in the classroom. In A. Elliot and C. Dweck (eds), *Handbook of Competence and Motivation*. New York: Guilford Press.

Urdan, T. and Mestas, M. (2006). The goals behind performance goals. *Journal of Educational Psychology*, 98(2), 354–65.

Valenzuela, A. (1999). *Subtractive Schooling: US-Mexican Youth and the Politics of Caring*. Albany: State University of New York Press.

Van Yperen, N.W., Elliot, A.J. and Anseel, F. (2009). The influence of mastery-avoidance goals on performance improvement. *European Journal of Social Psychology*, 39(6), 932–43.

Weeden, P., Winter, J. and Broadfoot, P. (2002). *Assessment: What's in it for Schools?* Abingdon: Routledge Falmer.

Wentzel, K.R. (1993). Motivation and achievement in early adolescence: The role of multiple classroom goals. *Journal of Early Adolescence*, 13(1), 4–20.

White, R.W. (1959). Motivation reconsidered: The concept of competence. *Psychological Review*, 66(5), 297–333.

Wiliam, D. (1992). Value-added Attacks: technical issues in reporting national curriculum assessments. *British Educational Research Journal*, 18(4), 329–41.

Wiliam, D. and Black, P. (1996). Meanings and Consequences: A basis for distinguishing formative and summative functions of assessment? *British Educational Research Journal*, 22(5), 537–48.

Wolters, C.A. (2004). Advancing achievement goal theory: Using goal structures and goal orientations to predict students' motivation, cognition, and achievement. *Journal of Educational Psychology*, 96(2), 236–50.

4
DISCUSSING SELF-DETERMINATION THEORY AND CONTEMPORARY EDUCATIONAL POLICY

> From our view, schools are not factories with an aim of producing a standardized product, but rather contexts to foster human development. Like all developmental processes, progress must be nurtured rather than force-fed, and that requires an understanding of the nutriments through which true growth occurs.
>
> (Ryan and Weinstein, 2009, p. 230)

Like goal theory, self-determination theory (SDT) has made a significant contribution to our understanding of motivation in the context of education. Recently, there have been significant efforts by SDT researchers to theoretically (Ryan and Brown, 2005; Ryan and Weinstein, 2009) and empirically (Wilkesmann and Schmid, 2014; Rogers and Tannock, 2013) address the issues that arise when we consider this popular motivational theory in relation to contemporary educational policy. As Ryan and Weinstein's (2009) quote suggests, it is time educational policy demonstrated a concern with better understanding and considering its impact upon psychological growth and well-being.

As this book has highlighted, numerous critics have written about the problems associated with educational policies such as high stakes testing. However, what is lacking is a theoretical and empirical basis for understanding these effects on people. As Ryan and Weinstein (2009) have noted, SDT offers both of these. Psychological critics of neoliberal policy (Carr and Batlle, 2015; Winegard and Winegard, 2011) have suggested that it will be particularly important that we are able to offer conceptually and empirically sound criticism of the ways in which economically oriented policy might damage people. To this end, comprehensive theoretical frameworks that facilitate the development of knowledge around which to organise such criticism will be important tools. This chapter first sketches out the main assumptions of SDT and subsequently discusses the issues that arise when we begin to explore the interface between the theory and trends in contemporary educational policy.

Self-determination theory and education

SDT (Deci and Ryan, 1985; Ryan and Deci, 2000) is best described as a macro-theory of human motivation, integrating a range of issues such as personality development, self-regulation, global psychological needs, non-conscious processes, the relations of culture to motivation and the impact of social environments on motivation, affect, behaviour and well-being (Deci and Ryan, 2008). A central assumption of SDT is the idea that people have a natural predilection toward the development of a unified sense of self (Ryan and Deci, 2004), striving to integrate within themselves new ideas and experiences that are encountered. That is, people are theorised to possess an innate curiosity, interest and love of learning (Niemiec and Ryan, 2009). However, SDT proposes that this predilection towards growth and actualisation by no means guarantees that people will attain it, and there are clear and identifiable social-contextual factors that have the potential to enhance or thwart its accomplishment. Hence, the SDT framework views growth and integration as heavily dependent upon the social-contextual provision of key psychological nutriments necessary to nourish actualisation (Ryan and Deci, 2004).

In basic needs theory, Ryan and Deci (2000) assert that psychological needs are specifiable requirements necessary for organisms to survive and thrive; withholding these needs 'will lead reliably to deterioration of growth and integrity, whereas making them available will lead to maintenance and enhancement' (p. 7). In other words, human needs are a way of helping us articulate the universal psychological requirements required for psychological health, well-being and effective functioning. The idea that people possess basic needs makes it important to understand how social contexts such as education can provide the conditions for them to satisfy these important psychological needs. That is, motivation, learning, empowerment, performance and development will be most likely when social contexts can support people's ability to satisfy these needs (Deci et al., 1999). The basic needs of competence, autonomy and relatedness have provided a framework for examining how social-contextual factors can enhance or inhibit psychological growth and actualisation.

Competence

The need for competence, also a core feature of human motivation in goal theory, reflects the innate propensity to experience a sense of efficacy and confidence in one's interactions with the surrounding environment (White, 1959), stimulating individuals to seek out challenges and to enhance and develop their capacities. Learners are likely to feel competent when they are able to meet the challenges and demands placed upon them in the context of their schoolwork and education.

Autonomy

As Ryan and Deci (2004) have articulated, autonomy is the need for individuals to 'experience their behaviour as an expression of the self, such that, even when actions are influenced by outside sources, the actors concur with those influences, feeling both initiative and value with regard to them' (p. 8). Deci and Ryan (2000) suggest that autonomy is satisfied when there is an internal perceived locus of causality (I-PLOC) and people feel as though they are both the origin and orchestrator of their behaviour.

Relatedness

The need for relatedness is closely tied to ideas (Bowlby, 1979/2005; Harlow, 1958) suggesting that humans have an inbuilt propensity to feel a psychological sense of connectedness and belonging to other human beings. This need reflects a deep-rooted desire to justify one's existence by feeling that one is integral and accepted by others.

The extent to which these basic needs are satisfied by given social contexts is a central component of SDT, hypothesised to be linked to the direction and persistence with which individuals engage in goal-directed behaviour (Hagger and Chatzisarantis, 2007). The needs are a central element of each of the SDT sub-theories.

Intrinsic motivation

Intrinsic motivation is the archetype of self-determined motivation. That is, intrinsically motivated activities 'are activities that people do naturally and spontaneously when they feel free to follow their inner interests' (Deci and Ryan, 2000, p. 234). Intrinsically motivated learners play, explore and engage in activities purely for the pleasure derived from doing so; the activity is an end in itself. The maintenance and development of intrinsic motivation have been linked with satisfaction of the basic psychological needs (Deci *et al.*, 1999; Ryan and Deci, 2007). In fact, SDT proposes (Deci and Ryan, 1980) that the basic needs are the 'necessary conditions for the maintenance and enhancement of intrinsic motivation' (Ryan and Deci, 2007, p. 3).

In the context of education, there have been numerous studies that have explored intrinsic motivation from an SDT perspective (Deci *et al.*, 1999; Niemiec and Ryan, 2009). In a compelling study, Deci *et al.* (1981) explored elementary school teachers' reported orientations towards controlling children's behaviour versus supporting their autonomy. Results identified that children who were assigned to an autonomy-supportive teacher demonstrated superior levels of intrinsic motivation, perceived competence and self-esteem over time. Furthermore, in American (Grolnick and Ryan, 1987) and Japanese (Kage and Namiki, 1990) schools, intrinsic motivation and performance in relation to educational activities have consistently been positively linked to autonomy-supportive environments and dampened by evaluative pressures.

Contemporary research has replicated these findings and continued to provide support for the importance of SDT's predictions around intrinsic motivation in educational contexts. For example, Tsai *et al.* (2008) identified that German school children showed significantly more intrinsic interest towards lessons in which teachers were autonomy-supportive. Their interest diminished in lessons where teachers were externally controlling. A similar finding was noted by Wilkesmann and Schmid (2014) in the context of German higher education. Specifically, they identified that professors' intrinsic motivation towards teaching in higher education was undermined by controlling accountability mechanisms and supported by a sense of social relatedness, competence and autonomy. In Canadian students, Burton *et al.* (2006) identified that intrinsic motivation was associated with psychological wellbeing and that this was independent of academic performance. Furthermore, Taylor *et al.* (2014) employed a meta-analysis of eighteen international studies exploring the relationship between intrinsic motivation and educational attainment, along with a series of controlled longitudinal studies: (a) the meta-analysis pointed towards the important role of intrinsic motivation in facilitating school achievement, and (b) the longitudinal explorations of students in Canada and Sweden suggested that intrinsic motivation was the only type of motivation to be consistently related to academic performance over a one year period. Taylor *et al.* (2014) concluded that 'our findings highlight the unique importance of intrinsic motivation for the future academic success of high school and college students' (p. 342). Niemiec and Ryan (2009) have contended that in educational research, it is difficult to dispute the weight of the evidence in support of the following facts: (a) students tend to learn, develop and perform better and more creatively when they are intrinsically motivated, and (b) that intrinsic motivation is best encouraged by an environment that supports autonomy, whereas it is undermined by controlling contexts (both of which are heavily linked to teachers' behaviour).

Extrinsic motivation and internalisation

Education, learning and teaching are not always fun, pleasurable and intrinsically satisfying. For example, not all young children are likely to find it intrinsically pleasurable to engage in the various assignments they are required by their teachers to undertake as 'homework' each evening, and students frequently focus solely upon producing what is required to satisfy a particular grade specification and have little intrinsic interest in the task. Clearly, beyond intrinsic motivation, there are other types of behaviour regulation that underpin individuals' motivation in educational contexts. SDT (Deci and Ryan, 1985) proposes a motivational continuum that conceptualises different forms of motivation ranging from highly autonomous (e.g. 'pure' intrinsic motivation) to highly controlling (i.e. 'pure' extrinsic motivation). This continuum also recognises that certain extrinsically motivated actions can sometimes become 'internally motivated' in the sense that they begin to serve internal rather than external goals (Ryan and Deci, 2007).

External regulation is the least self-determined form of motivation and reflects a behaviour that is undertaken purely as the means to an external end, such as a specific reward or because of pressures from external sources. For example, a student might work on a piece of coursework purely to earn a particular grade or to avoid a particular punishment. The problem with external regulation is that the behaviour is unlikely to be maintained once the reward or punishment is no longer available (Niemiec and Ryan, 2009). Next on the continuum is *introjected regulation*, which reflects behaviours that are carried out based upon self-imposed feelings of guilt or pressure, reflecting an internalised belief that one 'ought' to undertake a specific behaviour, not that they 'want' to (Wang et al., 2002). This motivational regulation moves beyond external regulation in the sense that it tends to reflect an *internalisation* of external pressures. This might involve a student striving to learn in order to avoid a sense of shame or to feel a sense of worthiness (Niemiec et al., 2008). A particular distinction between external and introjected regulations and more self-determined forms of motivation (such as intrinsic motivation) is the fact that they reflect an external perceived locus of control (E-PLOC), which originates from outside of the self. In essence, the behaviour is experienced as being *imposed* upon individuals (either by external forces or by the self).

Identified regulation is a more self-determined form of motivation and reflects behaviours that are undertaken because individuals consider them to be valuable or important. For example, a student may engage in the reading material necessary for a clinical psychology assignment because he/she believes that understanding the material will be important for his/her future experiences in the profession (but *not* because it is intrinsically or inherently pleasurable to do so). *Integrated regulation* is a more autonomous version of identified regulation in the sense that the valued and important behaviour has been internalised and connected with core aspects of the self. For example, the clinical psychology student above may be motivated to study the material because it connects with his/her core values to psychologically assist and care for others (and he/she recognises the task as clearly connecting with his/her values in this way). These forms of behavioural regulation are both more reflective of an I-PLOC because they originate much more strongly from core aspects of the self as opposed to external pressure and control.

Again, there is a significant body of work in education that has explored the psychological and academic consequences of these more autonomous motivational regulations and of the environmental conditions necessary to support them. For example, Grolnick, Ryan and Deci (1991) identified that elementary students who reported higher levels of the more autonomous regulations for learning were reported by their teachers as exhibiting higher attainment and adjustment in the classroom. Grolnick and Ryan (1987) demonstrated that elementary school students with more autonomous forms of motivation towards doing schoolwork were more likely to evidence greater conceptual learning and deeper understanding of the material. They (Grolnick and Ryan, 1987) also found that asking elementary students to learn material in order to be tested on it resulted in dampened interest and decreased conceptual learning than did asking students to learn the material without mentioning a test (the test condition led to short-term gains in rote recall that lasted less than a week). Furthermore, Niemiec et al. (2006) reported that high-school students who experienced more autonomous regulations towards school exhibited higher levels of positive well-being (e.g. life satisfaction) and lower levels of ill being (e.g. depression). More recently, Ullrich-French and Cox (2009) identified that physical education (PE) students with greater levels of more self-determined forms of motivation reported the highest levels of enjoyment, effort and value attached to physical activity and the lowest levels of worry in the context of PE.

Niemiec and Ryan (2009) have suggested that intrinsic motivation and more self-determined, autonomous forms of motivational regulation are essential if students are to maintain volition towards educational activities, learn better and maximise psychological well-being and personal growth. It has been important to better understand how these more autonomous forms of motivation can be encouraged and supported by educational environments. In their review, Niemiec and Ryan (2009) have suggested that students are unlikely to personally value or assign meaning to activities that:

- They are ultimately unable to master or understand or that fail to offer them the opportunity to challenge and expand themselves (satisfying the need for competence). If students do not feel that feedback and learning support genuinely facilitates a sense of efficacious growth, they are unlikely to attach value and importance to the activity.
- They feel coerced or pressured to engage in. That is, the activity genuinely needs to feel like it is something the learner is choosing to engage in and in which their voice and feelings are heard and valued (satisfying the need for autonomy).
- Do not enable them to connect and relate to people they genuinely feel respect and value them. People are more likely to value activities and integrate them within themselves when those activities facilitate a connection and sense of belonging to those with whom they have (or would like to have) a meaningful connection (satisfying the need for relatedness).

SDT has provided a strong conceptual and empirical basis for suggesting, as with intrinsic motivation, that supporting these basic psychological needs for competence, autonomy and relatedness matters in relation to internalising more autonomous forms of motivation. For example, Chirkov and Ryan (2001) identified that Russian and American students' perceptions of autonomy support from both parents and teachers were correlated positively with more autonomous, self-determined forms of academic motivation. Likewise, Ntoumanis (2001) identified that in British physical education, students' satisfaction of the basic psychological needs was associated with higher levels of more autonomous forms of motivation.

Self-determination theory and educational policy

The conceptual and empirical evidence from SDT in the context of education suggests that a system that values teachers' and learners' motivation, achievement and well-being ought to carefully consider the extent to which it provides a platform that supports (and does not thwart) basic psychological needs. Over fifteen years ago, Deci et al. (1999) suggested that it is clear from SDT that the degree to which teachers' behaviour is experienced by pupils as autonomy-supportive has an important influence on the development of motivation and well-being. It is therefore important to understand factors that might predispose teachers to adopt more controlling or autonomy-supportive behaviour. To this end, there is growing support for the idea that the external pressures placed upon teachers by educational policy may be a particularly problematic issue from a psychological and motivational perspective (Niemiec and Ryan, 2009; Ryan and Brown, 2005; Ryan and Weinstein, 2009).

Roth et al. (2007) identified that Israeli teachers who felt more controlled in relation to their professional lives were less autonomously supportive towards their students. Furthermore, Pelletier et al. (2002) revealed that Canadian teachers who identified that they experienced more pressure from above (in the form of imposed curricula and pressure to meet performance targets in their students) were less likely to be autonomy-supportive and more likely to be controlling towards their students. Niemiec and Ryan (2009) rationalised these findings in two ways: (a) teachers who feel pressured and controlled by policy from above are likely to experience dampened autonomy towards their work, resulting in motivational decrements that translate into lower levels of enthusiasm, energy and creativity being brought into the classroom to inspire and enthuse students, and (b) increasing pressure towards student attainment of outcomes (to which teachers are increasingly held accountable) means that extrinsic incentives such as grade specifications and externally imposed standards drown out the possibilities for other more motivating teaching practices. In Chapter 3, I discussed how researchers (Gleeson and Gunter, 2001) have documented a considerable shift in educational policy that has taken teachers from a position of 'relative autonomy' to a 'technical workforce' to be managed and controlled. There may be a heavy motivational price to pay for such an invasion and de-professionalisation of teaching.

A raft of controlling educational policies

The extent to which neoliberal educational policy has completely overlooked consideration for students' basic psychological needs is deeply concerning. In her scoping of the UK neoliberal policy context, Brown (2015) identified that the UK education reforms in 2011 were clearly born out of political discourse obsessed with 'underperforming pupils' and a 'state theory of learning' that has been described as:

> A highly regulated system in which performance can be measured quantitatively by test results. The attendant theory of motivation is that teachers and pupils will be driven to improve against the state determined performance targets. (Lauder, 2009, p. 200)

In a white paper, 'The Importance of Teaching' (DfE, 2010), the UK Coalition government's position on education reform identified 'poor behaviour in school' as one of the most significant factors felt to be holding back national education performance figures. The document subsequently devoted significant attention to strengthening the role of schools in imposing discipline on students (Brown, 2015). This was reflected in the words of the Prime Minister, David Cameron:

> There is no one step that can be taken, but we need a benefit system that rewards work and is on the side of families, we need more discipline in our schools, we need action to deal with the most disruptive families, and we need a criminal justice system that scores a clear and heavy line between right and wrong. In short, all action necessary to help mend our broken society. (Brown, 2015, p. 7)

Such discourse clearly guided educational policy reform and marked the beginning of what Brown (2015) described as a renewed 'militant approach' (p. 9) to raising educational standards under the Coalition government in the UK.

This militant approach to education was reflected in a raft of policies that sought to address the government's concern with strengthening schools' hand in relation to controlling young people's behaviour. As Brown (2015) has noted, it is perhaps no accident that the head of Ofsted at the time, Michael Wilshaw, was the former head of a deprived East London school who had led the school from the brink of failure to one of the country's highest performing academies. In an interview for *The Guardian* with Susanna Rustin (2011), Wilshaw's success was attributed to a strict authoritarian ethos that included measures such as strict adherence to school uniform policy, no 'special handshakes,' no large groups, no hugging, politeness to adults, detentions on Saturdays and restraining orders for unruly parents. Brown (2015) has suggested that this ethos clearly mirrored the approach adopted by the Secretary of State for Education, Michael Gove, whose guidelines for teachers (DfE, 2014) underlined the importance of measures such as 'screening and searching' young people and 'disciplining' pupils both inside and outside of school.

Policies that reflected this disciplinarian approach to education included the 'troops to teachers' programme. This programme offered teacher training routes for graduate and non-graduate military service leavers that would lead them to qualified teacher status. It included financial subsidies and a fast track route into teaching for former military service personnel (Brown, 2015) and was justified by Michael Gove in a press release as reflecting:

> A huge opportunity for those people who have served their country in uniform to serve their country in our schools. They have many of the virtues

that parents across the country feel have disappeared from our schools and need to be restored: self-discipline, a sense of purpose, and a belief in the importance of working as a team. (Brown, 2015, p. 11)

In her critique of this policy initiative, Brown (2015) questioned whether 'troops to teachers' might not be more aptly described as 'teachers to sergeants.' From this perspective, Brown (2015) has argued that the subtext of Gove's plans was that 'our classrooms are so out of control that drastic military action is called for' (p. 11). An illuminating quote presented from an ex-army teaching colleague about his opinions on the predominant purpose of military training was that 'you simply couldn't allow them to think for themselves' (Brown, 2015, p. 11). In her article in *The Guardian*, Francis Gilbert outlines the reasons why it is questionable to assume that the blind obedience required of army personnel is transferable to the classroom: 'in the military, independent thought can be fatal, whereas in schools it's absolutely crucial' (Should more ex-soldiers become teachers?).

The militant approach to education also extended into UK schoolchildren's social lives with the introduction of measures that sought to, as Brown (2015) has described, 'ban best friends'. That is, the desire to ensure that children prioritised their schoolwork above all else led some schools to attempt interventions that were effectively designed to 'limit' children's friendships so that they did not disrupt their focus on schoolwork. Brown (2015) noted how Russell Hobby, of the National Association of Head Teachers, confirmed that a number of schools in South West London and Surrey had introduced such measures in order to avoid children having best friends in favour of playing in large groups. In an interview with Marsden and Hough (2013), for *The Telegraph*, one head teacher suggested that:

There is sound judgment behind it. You can get very possessive friendships, and it is much easier if they share friendships and have a wide range of good friends rather than obsessing too much about who their best friend is. I would certainly endorse a policy which says we should have lots of good friends, not a best friend.

For Waiton (2008), such policy discourse reflects the essence of neoliberal politics: genuinely capturing people's hearts and minds is not the core objective and is bypassed by a framework that relies on punishments and sanctions seeking, instead, to govern people's lives.

Psychological critique of such policy

Psychology has much to offer the debate around the sorts of militant educational policies described above. There are compelling reasons to object to the sorts of disturbing discourse discussed above that ultimately seeks to invade and micromanage children's social lives and behaviour. For example, in relation to discourse around limiting children's friendships, Wubbels, den Brok, van Tartwijk and Levy (2012) have highlighted that the importance of interpersonal relationships in education has been recognised for some time. The psychiatrist, Harry Sullivan, outlined how the field of psychology '*is* the field of interpersonal relations . . . a personality can never be isolated from the complex of interpersonal relations in which the person lives and has his being' (Sullivan, 1940, p. 10). For Sullivan, people have a fundamental need for interpersonal relations and nothing is a more significant determinant of psychological well-being and quality of experience than the nature of our connections to the people around us.

With regard to peer relationships, research has consistently identified children's and adolescents' friendship quality as a critical determinant of an array of important outcomes such as general satisfaction with peer relations (Ladd, 1999), emotional health (Hartup, 1989), self-esteem (Keefe and Berndt, 1996), social anxiety (La Greca and Moore Harrison, 2005) and achievement (Parker and Gottman, 1989). Carr, Colthurst, Coyle and Elliott (2013) employed attachment theory to highlight the educational significance of young people being able to develop special, selective, unique attachment bonds, which Bowlby (1979/2005) identified as critical for the development and maintenance of psychological health through the lifespan. There is a wealth of support for the idea that individuals who are able to develop secure attachment relationships (i.e. a deep emotional connection with one or more attachment figures viewed as a genuine source of comfort in times of emotional distress and representing a base around which exploratory efforts and individuation can emerge) are more likely to feel that distress is manageable and less overwhelming, that they are not alone in the various stressors they might encounter, that others have inherently good intentions and that seeking social and emotional support in times of need is acceptable and valuable (Shaver and Mikulincer, 2002). Carr *et al.* (2013) identified that students who reported lower levels of secure attachment relationships in their lives were more likely to experience perceived loneliness, inhibited institutional integration, dampened psychological need satisfaction and depressive symptoms. Carr (2012) has noted that the close attachment bonds adolescents develop in the context of friendships may also be important ways for them to experience and develop key relational skills such as self-esteem enhancement, support, loyalty, intimacy and an ability to resolve conflict outside of the familial context.

Deep emotional bonds are an essential psychological resource throughout the lifespan. Rather than developing draconian policies that discourage the development of these deep emotional bonds, schools should be doing all that they can to promote them. Hazan and Shaver (1994) have argued that on a fundamental level, 'for an attachment to form there must be a strong force promoting closeness' (p. 11), which leads to relationship figures serving as a safe haven in times of distress and offering a secure base from which strong, special emotional ties can be formed (Hazan and Shaver, 1994; Trinke and Bartholomew, 1997).

In the context of SDT, self-determined forms of motivation are more likely to be elicited and sustained in conditions that foster the needs for competence, autonomy and relatedness. Consequently, factors that impact these psychological needs have the potential to limit the extent to which such forms of motivation are experienced in a given activity or context. Ryan and Deci (2006) have noted that 'because of the basic importance of the need for relatedness, people are highly motivated to be recognized or loved by others . . . yet parents, teachers, and peers often make their affection or regard contingent upon others' meeting their expectations or sharing their views' (p. 1567). The basic need to experience a sense of relatedness is likely to be undermined by policies that communicate to individuals that they are only positively regarded or valuable *if* they are able to learn and behave in a particular way.

Assor, Roth and Deci (2004) have viewed 'conditional regard' in education and parenting as a form of control or manipulation. In the context of parental relationships, they identified that parental use of conditional regard led to introjected regulation in children in relation to expected behaviours and undermined more autonomous forms of motivation. Children whose parents controlled them with the use of conditional regard had more fragile self-esteem, more transient satisfaction following successes, greater shame following failure and carried more significant feelings of rejection by and resentment towards their controlling parents (Assor *et al.*, 2004).

Over half a century ago, Carl Rogers (1959) sketched out a vision of the kind of education we might have if we sought to learn from the key principles allied to disciplines such as psychotherapy. He noted that one of the most significant principles of learning would be 'unconditional positive regard'. For Rogers (1959), this significant feature of the learning relationship in the context of a therapeutic alliance involves simply:

> A warm caring – a caring which is not possessive, which demands no personal gratification. It is an atmosphere which simply demonstrates 'I care'; not 'I care for you *if* you behave thus and so'. It involves as much feeling of acceptance for the client's expression of negative, 'bad', painful, fearful, and abnormal feelings, as for his expression of 'good', positive, mature, confident, and social feelings. It involves acceptance of and caring for the client as a separate person. To the degree that the therapist can provide this safety-creating climate of unconditional positive regard, significant learning is likely to take place. (Rogers, 1959, p. 234)

It is essential that we carefully discuss the extent to which policy shifts designed to micromanage young people's lives, scrutinising and sanctioning them when aspects of their lives and behaviour do not align with state defined ideals, are moving us away from a culture of unconditional positive regard in education. Frameworks such as SDT have the potential to help us understand the motivational and psychological consequences that such a culture might provoke and to weigh-in with substantiated and credible critique.

High stakes testing

In a discussion of the interface between educational policy and SDT, it would be remiss not to briefly mention high stakes testing. The SDT literature has begun to critique high stakes testing policy from a motivational perspective (Ryan and Brown, 2005; Ryan and Weinstein, 2009). Ryan and Weinstein (2009) have noted that advocates of high stakes testing policies (Finn, 1991) argue that rewards and sanctions (at school, teacher and pupil level) based upon test results are simply an example of an effective motivational technique grounded in classic behaviourist assumptions (Skinner, 1953). However, Ryan and Weinstein (2009) suggested that the fundamental distinction between high stakes testing policies and classic behaviourist principles is that behaviourism applies reinforcements to *behaviour* whereas contemporary testing policies have tended to make rewards and sanctions contingent upon *outcomes* (e.g. school, teacher or individual test results). Ryan and Brown (2005) identified some major problems with this line of thinking: (a) when outcomes alone are reinforced then it tends to be the case that *whatever* led to such outcomes is also reinforced and this has meant that both desirable (e.g. implementation of new teaching methods) *and* undesirable (e.g. teaching to the test, removal of low achievers from the pool) behaviours have been fostered, and (b) a myopic focus on a carrot and stick approach to motivate schools, teachers and pupils has ignored (and likely damaged) people's inner motivational worlds and intrinsic interest.

SDT's central propositions suggest that high stakes testing exerts pressure on teachers to transform teaching *content*. Ryan and Weinstein (2009) have outlined that when people's main motivation for a particular activity or event is a controlling system of rewards and sanctions, then they are likely to develop an extrinsic motivational focus and take the shortest route to the desired extrinsic end. In relation to high stakes testing, if test results become the carrot then it is unsurprising that high stakes testing will incite excessive test preparation strategies, such as: teaching to the test, a narrowing of the curriculum so that it is focused solely upon test-relevant material, removing low achievers from the pool of test-takers and micromanaging teaching environments. There is significant data to support these assumptions in high stakes testing environments, with evidence of all manner of unjust practices being fostered in the name of test results (Kohn, 2000; Nichols and Berliner, 2007). For example, Barksdale-Ladd and Thomas (2000) conducted in-depth interviews with fifty-nine US teachers on the subject of high stakes testing. The teachers confirmed that high stakes testing specifically invaded the content of their teaching. In addition to encouraging a focus upon test-relevant teaching methods, the teachers highlighted that high stakes testing had forced them to discontinue or dramatically reduce highly valued learning activities such as: (a) silent reading; (b) buddy reading and shared reading; (c) book talks; (d) collaborative writing and writing process; (e) science experiments; (f) picnics; (g) field trips; (h) classroom cooking; (i) classroom drama, choral reading and skits; (j) thematic, integrated instructional units; (k) creative activities (particularly creative, imaginative writing experiences); (l) games (math and reading); (m) manipulative mathematics

Discussing self-determination theory

experiences and (n) play-based breaks and recess. Below, I reproduce some of the quotes from the teachers in Barksdale-Ladd and Thomas's (2000) study. They are particularly emotive and illuminating:

> You wouldn't believe it. There were in-service meetings with the supervisor from the central office, about three of them, and then we met in grade-level teams once a week for months. Everybody gathered materials and made materials, and we shared them with each other, and we created all of these big three-ring binders full of things – things to do early in the year, things to do at holiday time. We created tons of practice tests because we wanted the kids using this type of test format all year long. I'll bet we spent 50 hours that first year. Preparing for that test took over our lives at first; then we got to see what the test was really like, and we spent more time next year. It is endless. *(Teacher 1)*

> I'm not the teacher I used to be. I used to be great, and I couldn't wait to get to school every day because I loved being great at what I do. All of the most powerful teaching tools I used to use every day are no good to me now because they don't help children get ready for the test, and it makes me like a robot instead of a teacher. I didn't need a college degree and a master's degree to do what I do now. They don't need real teachers to prepare children for tests and, in fact, I think they could just develop computer programs to do this. *(Teacher 2)*

> I know this is disrespectful, but these tests are making my kids stupid. The kids I've had the last few years have gotten higher scores because I've worked so hard at getting them ready for the tests, but this is a facade because they just don't have it together like my former students. They don't read as well because they're only reading for main ideas and supporting details and resolutions and characterizations which compared to my students a few years ago is a sin. Those students read for getting the whole picture and for fun. They loved reading. But these students, they just think reading is something you do for a test. Learning for the tests isn't meaningful; it's a chore, and so I think the tests have really made achievement go down . . . the scores are up, but the kids [today] know less, and they are less as people . . . I think it's a crime; it's educational malpractice. *(Teacher 5)*

> I would like to find out who wrote those standards and I'd like to force them to come to my school and sit in with my kids every day for a month. They'd change those standards, and they'd see that I'm a great teacher and my kids work hard . . . but they [kids] just aren't all ready for these standards. *(Teacher 8)*

Carl Rogers (1959) discussed the importance of 'the teacher's real-ness' (p. 237) in the educative process. He was referring to the idea that for a genuine learning relationship to develop, the teacher must be allowed to be the person that she is.

That is, she must be aware of the attitudes she holds, acceptant of her own feelings, enthusiastic about subjects she likes, bored by subjects she doesn't like, sometimes angry but also sensitive and sympathetic. Put differently, for Rogers (1959), a teacher 'is a *person*, not a faceless embodiment of a curricular requirement' (p. 237). Rogers's idea of 'teacher realness' resonates with Ryan and Deci's (2006) discussions about the importance of autonomy. Specifically, Ryan and Deci (2006) discussed the importance of authenticity in relation to autonomous behaviour, where behaviour is experienced as '*really* proceeding from its reputed author' (Ryan and Deci, 2006, p. 1561), endorsed by the self, fully identified with and owned (Ryan and Deci, 2006). The quotes from the teachers in Barksdale-Ladd and Thomas's (2000) study speak clearly to the struggles teachers are currently facing to bring 'realness' into the classroom, particularly in the face of policies such as high stakes testing.

Rogers' (1959) was unclear about *why* he saw teacher 'realness' as an important part of 'good' education. To this end, in SDT a framework exists for better understanding the motivational and psychological consequences (for teachers *and* pupils) of enabling or thwarting teacher 'realness'. In the context of SDT, Ryan and Deci (2006) have identified the most significant psychological and behavioural consequences of a lack of authenticity and autonomy. These include:

- *Performance and Creativity* – Undermining autonomous forms of motivation has consistently been linked to performance decrements, especially where creative, flexible or complex tasks are to be performed (Ryan and Deci, 2006; Utman, 1997).
- *Relationship Quality* – Autonomy support has been strongly linked to the development of human attachment bonds and their psychological consequences. For example, La Guardia, Ryan, Couchman and Deci (2000) identified that, in a given relationship, when a relational partner is experienced as autonomy-supportive then there is an increased likelihood that a sense of attachment security in the relationship will be enhanced. Hence, individuals are more likely to experience a relational partner as a secure base and safe haven if they perceive that it is acceptable to authentically be the person they are in the context of the relationship. Ryan *et al.* (2005) have also shown that seeking emotional support in the context of a relationship is also linked to the extent to which the other is perceived to be autonomy-supportive.
- *Psychopathology and Well-being* – As Ryan *et al.* (2006) have also demonstrated, disturbances in relation to the basic need for autonomy and authenticity have been consistently linked to psychopathology. Highly controlling social contexts have been implicated in the development of such psychopathology too. Ryan and Deci (2006) have suggested that healthy psychological functioning is heavily dependent upon the need to experience a sense of autonomy.

As Ryan and Deci (2006) noted:

> Given the pervasive effects of variations in both the experience of autonomy and the social conditions that either support or thwart it, it seems undeniable

that autonomy is a central human concern . . . But in 'real' life people often feel they cannot be autonomous. Social controls, evaluative pressures, rewards and punishments can powerfully constrain or entrain behavior, sometimes outside awareness. (p. 1566)

According to Foucault, it has been the neoliberal modus operandi to attempt to structure individual behaviour and social relations in accordance with economic rationality. As I noted in Chapter 1, it has become obvious that the pursuit of economic ideals cannot take place without states attempting to modify human beings' lives in accordance with market values. This modus operandi is reflected in the educational policies described and discussed above. Government reactions to perceived underperformance in relation to state-determined national attainment targets have often been to identify young people's behaviour or attainment as a social/individual factor to be controlled in order to redress perceived problems. Subsequently, schools have been identified as the institutions charged with enforcing the necessary control, and an array of controlling policies has been introduced. However, as also noted in Chapter 1, a key problem is that human beings frequently resist such policy movements because people are not meant to be governed in accordance with an ultimately economic rationality (Polanyi, 1944; Robertson, 2007).

It is critical for critics to articulate *why* and *how* it may be damaging to people to organise and conceptualise them this way. One possibility is that a policy that prioritises market-based considerations over and above people could be significantly damaging to individuals on a psychological level (Winegard and Winegard, 2011). As Winegard and Winegard (2011) have noted, it is only through better understanding the effects of such policies on real human beings that we are critical of them. Accordingly, there is an urgent need to evaluate the extent to which the sorts of controlling, invasive policy initiatives identified above are detrimental to people's learning and psychological well-being and, if we think that they are, we must speak out against them. As has been discussed in this section, from a psychological perspective, it seems logical to suggest that policies seeking to position teaching as a controlling and invasive endeavour risk undermining important aspects of motivation and well-being outlined in SDT. SDT knowledge and research has the potential to make a significant contribution to our efforts to expose the injustices inherent in such educational policy.

The erosion of pluralism (or motivational discrimination)

In the context of SDT, Ryan and Weinstein (2009) have argued that one of the most significant effects of high stakes testing policies is that they have fostered a more standardised curriculum in order to ensure that all students receive an education of the same quality and that the curriculum aligns with a narrow spectrum of imposed national standards. One of the many concerns around such uniformity has been that the one-size-fits-all approach to assessment (and its associated test-relevant curricula) has significantly eroded pluralism in relation to teaching and learning. For Ryan and Weinstein (2009), this has likely caused significant problems for diverse groups of young people. From one perspective, they have argued that such a uniform approach to standards and curricula has meant that few students are optimally challenged. For example, they argued that for gifted children such an approach to education is frequently 'irrelevant, limiting, and boring' (p. 229) whereas students with language or learning barriers might often find it 'inappropriate or demoralising' (p. 229).

From a motivational perspective, one of the central concerns about a one-size-fits-all approach to education (and a lack of plurality) is that certain populations of children and young people may be particularly disadvantaged. That is, perhaps the current rigid imposition of curriculum and assessment is motivationally disadvantageous for certain groups for whom the current system is unsuitable or irrelevant. For example, Timimi and his colleagues (Timimi, 2002, 2005; Timimi and Radcliffe, 2005; Timimi and Leo, 2006) have written extensively about children with ADHD diagnoses. They have suggested that the contemporary political context has been loaded with anxieties surrounding control of unruly children, and teachers, parents and children have been pressured towards viewing non-conformity to a myopic set of learning practices and behavioural norms as 'pathological'. Furthermore, they argued that this has been an ideal cultural platform for the normalisation of concepts such as ADHD (Timimi, 2002). Indeed, there has been a clear correlation between political mandates within educational policy and rates of diagnosis of such disorders (Fulton *et al.*, 2009). As Timimi and Radcliffe (2005) noted:

> ADHD is now firmly entrenched in the cultural expectations of our education system. The defining of a disability requiring special needs help at school is now shaped by the disciplines of medicine and psychology (Hey *et al.*, 1998). The adherence of these two fields to measuring physical and mental competence in order to determine normality inevitably conveys assumptions about deviance and failure and these labels then become attached to both individuals and groups who have failed to measure up/conform. Special needs practice in schools rests on within-child explanations. (p. 13)

Of particular concern for critics has been the idea that, within such a system, children with an ADHD diagnosis quickly become the objects of their descriptive diagnosis. Subsequently, there is a risk that they are more likely to be alienated from educational contexts and that their individuality, creativity and capacity to demonstrate something exceptional, different and alternative may be more likely to go unnoticed (Timimi and Radcliffe, 2005). Timimi and Radcliffe (2005) argued that, 'ADHD pushes teachers, parents and medical practitioners into self-doubt about their capacity to teach and care for children. The opportunities for developing reflexive, appreciative child management practices and skills are lost' (p. 13). That is, the normalisation of ADHD in the classroom has encouraged us to abandon the pursuit of a diverse, inclusive, individualised approach to teaching and learning, enabling us to rationalise as 'medical' the failure of certain children to learn effectively in an alarmingly one-dimensional education system.

Recently, researchers have recognised that SDT offers a motivational lens through which to explore such issues. For example, Rogers and Tannock (2013) recently examined the experiences of children with high versus low levels of ADHD symptoms in relation to perceived levels of basic need satisfaction in the classroom. A sample of Canadian children reported the extent to which they felt that their needs for autonomy (e.g. 'I can pretty much be myself in class'), relatedness (e.g. 'I feel that my teacher understands me') and competence (e.g. 'I have been able to learn interesting skills in class') were supported in the classroom. Results indicated that the children in the ADHD group reported experiencing their classrooms as more controlling, feeling less valued and cared about by their teachers and having higher levels of perceived incompetence in relation to learning. Rogers and Tannock (2013) suggested that the very nature of contemporary Western classroom settings requires children to engage with learning and teaching that is completely contrary to the nature of ADHD children, which may have a considerable impact on the extent to which such children are able to feel that their basic needs are supported (and/or the extent to which teachers feel able to provide for their needs). They argued that there is an urgent need to explore whether and how such motivational deficits in relation to the basic psychological needs of ADHD children unfold.

Of course, data such as that reported by Rogers and Tannock (2013) might equally be viewed as further evidence of the psychological 'deficits' in children 'suffering from' ADHD (i.e. perhaps motivational deficiencies are an additional symptom of an 'endogenous' disorder). However, it would be remiss to individualise these motivational deficits *without* considering and exploring other arguments. One possibility is that factors such as the lack of plurality and increasing rigidity fostered by policies such as high stakes testing (Ryan and Weinstein, 2009) discriminates against these children in a *motivational* sense, making it significantly more difficult for them to secure the psychological nutriments necessary to nurture more autonomous forms of motivation and a sense of enthusiasm, warmth and achievement in the classroom. Further research is necessary in order to explore important questions such as (a) whether deficits in psychological need satisfaction in children with ADHD translate into motivational deficits in relation to autonomous regulation and associated cognitive, affective and behavioural outcomes, and (b) whether such a motivational deficit exists in alternative educational contexts that encourage plurality and where teachers are less restricted by educational policy such as high stakes testing.

There are other groups of children and young people who may be significantly motivationally disadvantaged by an education system that seeks to impose a one-size-fits-all approach to learning. For example, in her book, *The Educational Binds of Poverty*, Brown (2015) presented detailed ethnographic accounts of the educational penalties incurred by children from highly mobile families, where moving schools was common due to factors such as community re-housing, familial redundancies or being part of traveller families. Brown (2015) identified that such children's educational outcomes were significantly hindered because of a number of 'educational binds'. Of particular concern was that data highlighted the enormous difficulties mobile children faced in relation to establishing warm, meaningful social connections with peers and teachers in school that made them feel valued and cared about. This was particularly challenging in the context of a lifestyle that involved frequent severance of existing bonds in 'old schools' and the need to re-establish them in new ones. These issues were often confounded by the fact that schools and teachers tended immediately to be focused upon such children's behaviour in relation to test-relevant learning practices and attainment rather than how best to support the establishment of key psychological needs that might support their enthusiasm and motivation for learning (e.g. such as a sense of relatedness and connection).

From an SDT perspective, it might be suggested that such children have unique needs in relation to establishing an educational environment that enables a sense of relatedness, autonomy and competence. However, if schools wish to inject the enthusiasm and autonomous regulation for education that would ultimately support such children's attainment and well-being then it would seem important to develop a policy that considers this. However, Brown (2015) noted that the current one-dimensional educational offering in the UK meant that heads and teachers alike were ill-equipped to take measures that genuinely supported the psychological needs of such children. Similarly, Lipman's (2004) ethnography of schools in Chicago identified that schools' and teachers' creativity in relation to teaching literacy to immigrant pupils was frequently undermined by pressure to teach to standardised tests. Lipman (2004) outlined a clear conflict between teachers feeling able to help pupils develop knowledge and skills that would cater for the genuine needs and concerns of their pupils and the development of knowledge and skills that would help them pass the standardised tests.

There may be particularly interesting motivational comparisons to be made with education systems that actively foster plurality. For example, Sahlberg (2011, 2015) has noted that one of the peculiarities of the Finnish education system is that governance is highly decentralised. The 320 municipalities have significant freedom to arrange schooling in accordance with local circumstances and the system is customised, from school to school, in accordance with local needs and situations. As Sahlberg (2011) has noted:

> The Finnish example suggests that a critical condition for attracting the most able young people is that teaching be an independent and respected profession rather than just a technical implementation of externally mandated standards and tests. Teachers' strong competence and preparedness are the prerequisites for the professional autonomy that makes teaching a valued career. (p. 38)

Additionally, Sahlberg (2015) recently commented on allegations that there is a lack of concern by Finnish educators about the fact that Finnish test scores have declined in relation to international rankings:

> Educators in Finland think, quite correctly, that schools should teach what young people need in their lives rather than try to bring national test scores back to where they were.

Furthermore, Finland's National Curriculum Framework for 2016 requires that students be involved in the planning of phenomenon-based study periods and that they must have input in assessing what they have learned. Such measures are a significant move towards the decentralisation of teaching and learning. From an SDT perspective, it may be particularly useful to explore the extent to which learner and teacher motivation are positively shaped around such policy movements, especially in comparison to systems that completely overlook such autonomy.

There is a need to examine and critique the extent to which neoliberal educational policy is fostering an education system that is motivationally disadvantageous to certain social groups. As Ryan and Weinstein (2009) noted, schools should be contexts that foster optimal human development and support individuals' basic psychological needs. Motivational equality is an essential aim if we are to promote in all students a genuine enthusiasm for learning and accomplishment and a sense of volition in relation to the educational enterprise. It is vital that we develop a theoretical and empirical base from which to better understand the extent to which certain educational policies such as high stakes testing are creating an uneven motivational playing field. To this end, exploring how certain groups are disadvantaged in the context of an SDT framework is a particularly fruitful avenue for future research.

Autonomy, agency and choice

In the context of SDT and beyond, there are important discussions to be had around the meaning of terms such as autonomy, agency and choice for policymakers, schools and teachers. In the last chapter, I discussed the importance for motivational psychologists of carefully considering the extent to which our theories, constructs and knowledge might be employed simply to pursue controlling educational goals under a more 'motivationally acceptable' pretext. In this sense, the idea was discussed that motivational science could simply become another tool for disciplinary power seeking ever more creative and 'legitimate' ways to strategically program individuals' activity (Foucault, 2008; Prilleltensky, 2008). It is important for SDT researchers and policymakers to be mindful of how terms such as autonomy come to be understood and are embedded in educational practice.

First, it is important to note the relationship between choice and autonomy. Researchers (Ntoumanis, 2001; Vallerand and Losier, 1999) have suggested that a teacher who provides choice in relation to educational activities is more likely to foster a sense of autonomy in the classroom. However, Ryan and Deci (2006) have warned that autonomy in the context of SDT should not be thought of as *synonymous* with choice provision (although, under certain conditions, choice can clearly foster a sense of autonomy). As Ryan and Deci (2006, p. 1576) noted, 'one can have many options and not feel autonomy . . . one could have only one option (which functionally means no choice) and yet feel quite autonomous so long as one truly endorses that option'. In essence, an important point to remember is that choice, so long as it is felt to be congruent with the self, can facilitate self-determination, especially when it aligns with that which individuals wholeheartedly endorse. However, number of available options is not a synonym for autonomy (Deci and Ryan, 1985). In this sense, policymakers should be careful not to presume that simple provision of choice in relation to how individuals go about pursuing the same instrumental educational goals automatically indicates autonomy-supportive educational practice. According to SDT, a system genuinely concerned with fostering autonomy *must* involve support for learning experiences that are perceived by individuals to be congruent with the self and fully identified with – *not* simply the provision of choice about how to go about pursuing externally imposed goals.

In his discussion about the usefulness of autonomy as a legitimate educational goal, Hand (2006) discussed the notion of 'circumstantial autonomy', which he took to reflect the extent to which a person's circumstances enable her to be free to determine her own actions. That is, she is said to lack such autonomy when she is 'deprived of such freedom, when she is enslaved, imprisoned or otherwise obliged to submit to the direction of others' (p. 537). For Hand (2006), circumstantial autonomy is the polar opposite of 'circumstantial heteronomy', which he defines as 'being obliged by one's circumstances to submit to the will of others' (p. 537). Hand (2006) has refuted the idea that circumstantial autonomy can be an educational goal in and of itself:

> Now I have no quarrel with the view that circumstantial autonomy is a desirable state of being. But it should be quite clear that it is a state of being one cannot confer on a person by *educating* her. What a person lacks when she lacks circumstantial autonomy cannot be imparted by teaching or acquired by learning. The deficiency lies not in her character but in the conditions under which she lives. The aim of increasing circumstantial autonomy by liberating people from restrictive or dictatorial social arrangements is coherent and worthwhile; but it is a political aim, not an educational one. (p. 537)

In this book, I disagree with Hand's (2006) contention that circumstantial autonomy is not an educational goal. I contend that circumstantial autonomy *is* an important educational goal because education *is* political and the ways in which individuals are 'governed' in the context of education can have a significant impact on their autonomy and associated well-being. We may not be able to confer circumstantial autonomy *upon* a person. However, we *can* aim to increase it by considering, developing and nurturing educational policies that genuinely seek to liberate people from restrictive educative processes that are not personally meaningful and oblige or persuade them to learn and develop within the parameters of a program of neoliberal governmentality.

What is more, I believe that circumstantial autonomy is a worthy aim for systems of education *because* such autonomy provides the platform upon which Hand's (2006) ideas related to 'dispositional autonomy' (another educational aim to which he objects) can be best nurtured and developed. For Hand (2006), dispositional autonomy moves beyond situational circumstances and reflects individuals' inclination and ability to determine and pursue their actions and desires. Aviram and Assor (2010) have used SDT as a basis for defending the importance of constructs closely aligned with dispositional autonomy for both socio-political and psychoethical reasons:

> If asked why commitment to autonomy is so important, the Millean liberal can come up with two categories of answers relating to social and political philosophy, or to ethics and psychology:
>
> 1 The social political answers:
>   - because without the enhancement of autonomy, Liberal Democracy has no raison d'être;
>   - because without it, Liberal Democracy might be a democracy, but not a liberal one (i.e. not honouring individuals' rights to freedom and dignity).
> 2 The ethical psychological answers:
>   - because self-knowledge is the best guarantee for (authentic) self-expression;
>   - because both self-expression and self-direction are the best guarantees we have for promising people a satisfying life. (p. 119)

As has been discussed in this chapter, psychological research in the realms of SDT has provided a wealth of evidence in support of the idea that seeking to foster human autonomy is an educational goal that aligns with the enhancement of human development, motivation and well-being (Aviram and Assor, 2010).

Furthermore, in relation to circumstantial autonomy, Patrick (2013) has endorsed the idea that genuine autonomy also involves 'agency' in relation to the system within which one is educated. From Patrick's (2013) perspective, individual agency is about the possibility to resist 'strong social suggestion through locating a position and role within social practice which is consistent with individual subjectivity and identity' (Billett, 2010, p. 12). She has argued that in order for individuals' behavioural regulation towards education to be truly autonomous then there must be a consideration of the extent to which educational life involves opportunities for 'practices of liberation' (Bevir, 1999, p. 65). That is, autonomy may also be heavily linked to *creating* and *fighting* for the circumstantial autonomy from which personal forms of autonomy arise.

In relation to this, Sonu's (2012) recent research raises interesting issues. Her ethnographic exploration of a US high school demonstrated how teachers and students, in the face of increasingly controlling school practices, 'performed' according to the 'public transcript' of neoliberal school culture, yet behind the scenes, in 'private spaces' not under surveillance, they critiqued, inserted and reclaimed their individual values in relation to what mattered. Sonu (2012) described 'the growing frustration among educators and students who find their imaginings for social justice largely unmet, if not deliberately crushed, in the public school classroom', where teachers and students 'keenly assess the degree of surveillance and therein create hidden private spaces where freedom and resistance may grow' (p. 241). In the midst of an increasingly controlling education system, it is interesting to discuss the extent to which teachers and students have a natural propensity towards feeling as though what they are doing is congruent with their core values and whether creation of the private spaces of resistance is a reflection of how they doggedly hang on to autonomy in the face of a system that increasingly edges it out. As Sonu (2012) has noted:

> Behind closed doors individuals have always spoken back to the structures and systems they find oppressive and in turn, produce spaces within which to release frustration over institutions deemed untrustworthy, unsafe, or unsympathetic. If performance is accepted as part of the educational world, perhaps even more applicable to those pressured by rigid and uniform curricular standards, then hidden transcripts may serve to frame resistance in a way that sees agency as sustained ritualized acts that refashion the dominant order no matter how visible or hidden. The concept of hidden transcripts then expands agency to include individuals who, behind the eyes and ears of school administration, critique its universalizing intention and refuse to submit to absolutes. (p. 256)

On the neoliberal educational landscape perhaps autonomy and agency are nurtured and discovered less and less in the realms of the 'public', 'performed' dimensions of educational life. Perhaps it will be in the hidden, private spaces of 'resistance' where individuals are truly able to find a sense of autonomy and agency on the neoliberal educational landscape. Perhaps individuals' dogged desire to hang on to their autonomy is a cry for help from those with the power to liberate. Perhaps SDT's privilege in relation to expertise, knowledge and legitimate authority is a noteworthy place to begin.

On this note, there have been interesting developments in the political psychology literature (Klar and Kasser, 2009) that have sought to incorporate SDT into the study of political activism and people's struggle to locate a sense of agency and autonomy in the face of oppression. Klar and Kasser (2009) drew upon Aristotle in order to make the case that when people engage in political activity, they are expressing a basic motive fundamental to being human. That is, they are actively making meaning out of their lives and expressing who they *really* are (this closely aligns with SDT's idea of autonomy discussed above). Aristotle asked 'which way of life is the more desirable – to join with other citizens and share in the state's activity, or to live in it like an alien, absolved from the ties of political society?' (350 BC/1948, p. 283). Accordingly, Klar and Kasser (2009) used Aristotle's logic to hypothesise that the extent to which people engage in political activism as an expression of their core beliefs and values might be positively associated with their well-being (or in Aristotle's terms – *eudaimonia*). They also related this to Erikson's (1950) ideas around the importance of *generativity* for health and well-being through the lifespan. Generativity, for Erikson, is closely linked to political activism in the sense that it reflects a 'desire to care about something bigger than the self and to foster the welfare of future generations' (Klar and Kasser, 2009, p. 756).

In a series of studies, Klar and Kasser (2009) found (a) that indicators of political activism were positively associated with measures of hedonic (e.g. life satisfaction, positive affect) and eudaimonic (e.g. meaning in life, self-actualisation, basic psychological need satisfaction, hope and agency) well-being, and (b) that there may be initial evidence of a *causal* link (experimental exposure to activist behaviour elicited higher levels of subjective vitality than exposure to non-activist or control conditions) between these variables. In relation to SDT, the authors concluded that activists are more likely to experience the satisfaction of basic psychological needs and that well-being may be significantly linked to the extent to which people are able to live lives that involve contributing to the political struggle towards what they truly believe in.

It is intriguing to reflect upon what this might *mean* in the context of SDT research in relation to education, social justice and well-being. Prilleltensky (2008) has called for psychologists and social scientists to increase their awareness of the relationship between power, oppression, liberation and wellness. It is interesting to speculate that perhaps the most significant contribution we might make towards supporting people's rights to experience their basic psychological needs in the context of education might be to help them fight and struggle *against* the oppressive forces and systems in which they are currently required to learn and educate. This is a radical departure from trying to 'tinker with' the individual in order to manage their motivational characteristics *within* such forces and systems. In essence, it is critical for SDT researchers to reflect upon what we wish to *do* with our knowledge. Who is it for and why? Paulo Freire (2000) noted the need to carefully consider the extent to which science, despite its claims toward value neutrality, is frequently a facilitator of oppressive regimes, where it has all too often been complacent and abdicated responsibility for such issues:

> the oppressor, in order to dominate, tries to deter the drive to search, the restlessness, and the creative power which characterize life, it kills life. More and more, the oppressors are using science and technology as unquestionably powerful instruments for their purpose: the maintenance of the oppressive

order through manipulation and repression. The oppressed, as objects, as 'things', have no purposes except those their oppressors prescribe for them. (p. 60)

In a strong critique, Lorenz (2012) made a convincing case for why some of the key features of neoliberal logic that have hijacked education are reminiscent of state Communism. He has argued that in many senses the neoliberal educational landscape reflects a 'privatized version of economic and bureaucratic totalitarianism' (Lorenz, 2012, p. 629): (1) like communism, the new language of managerialism is totalitarian in the sense that it leaves no institutionalised room for criticism or debate; (2) there has been a movement towards the permanent control, monitoring and surveillance of educational employees that has fostered a culture of pervasive mistrust and (3) the question of whether managers really do spend taxpayers' money more efficiently and whether the system is more reliable without the layer of management cannot be asked.

A particularly important question for SDT researchers, who have a significant contribution to make to discussions about the place of autonomy in education, is the extent to which a genuine support for personal autonomy can ever be fostered upon a platform that increasingly resembles totalitarianism (arguably the enemy of personal autonomy and agency). Furthermore, it will be important to consider whether motivational science wishes to become the study of 'working out ways to make people feel reasonably autonomous' in the midst of a system built around totalitarian principles that reflect the archetypal opposite of circumstantial autonomy.

Conclusion

A social justice perspective emphasises societal concerns (Vera and Speight, 2003), including issues such as equality, self-determination, interdependence and social responsibility (Bell, 1997; Vera and Speight, 2003). Vera and Speight (2003) have suggested that psychologists have traditionally been socialised into seeing themselves as apolitical. In the context of SDT, social justice may not typically have been the starting point for researchers. Nonetheless, as this chapter has sought to highlight, the theory holds potential to contribute significantly to the development of a knowledge base in motivational psychology equipped to critique, challenge and provide alternatives to educational policy and practice that some have considered unjust. As Louis *et al.* (2014) have noted, psychologists are advantaged by 'expertise' in relation to theorising, understanding and developing knowledge that seeks to identify political and institutional assumptions and practices that are unjust and falsifiable – we *can* pursue a social justice agenda. To this end, SDT offers those who seek to interrogate and critique neoliberal educational policy a theoretical platform from which to articulate and investigate the psychological consequences of such policy upon individuals. It is only through better understanding the effects of the neoliberal educational landscape on real human beings that we can be genuinely critical.

References

Allen, A. (2012). Cultivating the myopic learner: The shared project of high-stakes and low-stakes assessment. *British Journal of Sociology of Education*, 33, 641–59.
Aristotle. (1948). *The politics of Aristotle*, translated by B. Ernest. Oxford, UK: The Clarendon Press.
Assor, A., Roth, G. and Deci, E.L. (2004). The emotional costs of parents' conditional regard: A self-determination theory analysis. *Journal of Personality*, 72(1), 47–88.
Aviram, A. and Assor, A. (2010). In defence of personal autonomy as a fundamental aim of education in liberal democracies: A response to hand. *Oxford Review of Education*, 36(1), 111–26.
Barksdale-Ladd, A.M. and Thomas, K.F. (2000). What's at stake in high-stakes testing? Teachers and parents speak out. *Journal of Teacher Education*, 51(5), 384–97.
Bell, L.A. (1997). Theoretical foundations for social justice education. In M. Adams, L.A. Bell and P. Griffin (eds), *Teaching for Diversity and Social Justice: A Sourcebook* (pp. 3–15). New York: Routledge.
Bevir, M. (1999). Foucault and critique: deploying agency against autonomy. *Political Theory*, 27(1), 65–84.
Billett, S. (2010). Lifelong learning and self: work, subjectivity and learning. *Studies in Continuing Education*, 32(1), 1–16.
Bowlby, J. (1979/2005). *The Making and Breaking of Affectional Bonds* (1st edn, 1979/2nd edn, 2005). New York: Routledge.
Brown, C. (2015). *Educational Binds of Poverty: The Lives of School Children*. Abingdon, Oxon: Routledge.
Burton, K.D., Lydon, J.E., D'Alessandro, D.U. and Koestner, R. (2006). The differential effects of intrinsic and identified motivation on well-being and performance: Prospective, experimental, and implicit approaches to self-determination theory. *Journal of Personality and Social Psychology*, 91(4), 750–62.
Carr, S. (2012). *Attachment in Sport, Exercise and Wellness*. Abingdon, Oxon: Routledge.
Carr, S., Colthurst, K., Coyle, M. and Elliot, D. (2012). Attachment dimensions as predictors of mental health and psychosocial well-being in the transition to university. *European Journal of Psychology of Education*, 28(2), 157–72.
Carr, S. and Batlle, I.C. (2015). Attachment theory, neoliberalism, and social conscience. *Journal of Theoretical and Philosophical Psychology*, 35(3), 160–76.
Chirkov, V.I. and Ryan, R.M. (2001). Parent and teacher autonomy-support in Russian and U.S. Adolescents: common effects on well-being and academic motivation. *Journal of Cross-Cultural Psychology*, 32(5), 618–35.
Deci, E.L., Betley, G., Kahle, J., Abrams, L. and Porac, J. (1981). When trying to win: Competition and intrinsic motivation. *Personality and Social Psychology Bulletin*, 7(1), 79–83.
Deci, E.L. and Ryan, R.M. (1980). The empirical exploration of intrinsic motivational processes. In L. Berkowitz (ed.), *Advances in Experimental Social Psychology* (Vol. 13, pp. 39–80). New York: Academic Press.
Deci, E.L. and Ryan, R.M. (1985). *Intrinsic Motivation and Self-Determination in Human Behavior*. New York: Plenum.
Deci, E.L. and Ryan, R.M. (2000). The 'What' and 'Why' of goal pursuits: Human needs and the self-determination of behavior. *Psychological Inquiry*, 11(4), 227–68.
Deci, E.L., Vallerand, R.J., Pelletier, L.G. and Ryan, R.M. (1991). Motivation and education: The self-determination perspective. *Educational Psychologist*, 26(3), 325–46.
Department for Education. (2010). *The Importance of Teaching: The Schools White Paper*. Available at www.gov.uk/government/uploads/system/uploads/attachment_data/file/175429/CM-7980.pdf [Accessed 13 January 2015].

Department for Education. (2014). *Behaviour and Discipline in Schools: Advice for Headteachers and School Staff.* Available at www.gov.uk/government/publications/behaviour-and-discipline-in-schools [Accessed 12 January 2015].
Erikson, E.H. (1950). *Childhood and Society.* New York: Norton.
Finn, C. (1991). *We Must Take Charge: Our Schools and Our Future.* New York: Free Press.
Foucault, M. (2008). *The Birth of Biopolitics: Lectures at the Collège de France, 1978–1979*, translated by G. Burchell. In A.I. Davidson (ed.), New York: Palgrave Macmillan.
Freire, P. (2000). *Pedagogy of the Oppressed.* London: Bloomsbury Publishing.
Gilbert, F. (2010). Should more ex-soliders become teachers? *The Guardian*, 24 November 2010. Available at www.theguardian.com/theguardian/commentisfree/2010/nov/24/soldiers-teachers-michael-gove [Accessed 11 January 2015].
Gleeson, D. and Gunter, H. (2001). The performing school and the modernisation of teachers. In D. Gleeson and C. Husbands (eds), *The Performing School.* London: Routledge, Falmer.
Grolnick, W.S., Ryan, R.M. and Deci, E.L. (1991). Inner Resources for School Achievement: Motivational Mediators of Children's Perceptions of their Parents. *Journal of Educational Psychology*, *83*(4), 508–17.
Grolnick, W.S. and Ryan, R.M. (1987). Autonomy in children's learning: An experimental and individual difference investigation. *Journal of Personality and Social Psychology*, *52*(4), 890–98.
Hagger, M. and Chatzisarantis, N. (2007). *Intrinsic Motivation and Self-Determination In Exercise and Sport.* Champaign, IL: Human Kinetics.
Hand, M. (2006). Against autonomy as an educational aim. *Oxford Review of Education*, *32*(4), 535–50.
Harlow, H.E. (1958). The Nature of Love. *American Psychologist*, *13*(12), 673–85.
Hartup, W.W. (1989). Behavioral manifestations of children's friendships. In T.J. Berndt and G.W. Ladd (eds), *Peer Relationships in Child Development* (pp. 46–70). New York: Wiley.
Hazan, C. and Shaver, P.R. (1994). Attachment as an organizational framework for research on close relationships. *Psychological Inquiry*, *5*(1), 1–22.
Kage, M. and Namiki, H. (1990). The effects of evaluation structure on children's intrinsic motivation and learning. *Japanese Journal of Educational Psychology*, *38*(1), 36–45.
Keefe, K. and Berndt, T.J. (1996). Relations of friendship quality to self-esteem in early adolescence. *Journal of Early Adolescence*, *16*(1), 110–29.
Klar, M. and Kasser, T. (2009). Some benefits of being an activist: Measuring activism and its role in psychological well-being. *Political Psychology*, *30*(5), 755–77.
Kohn, A. (2000). Burnt at the high-stakes. *Journal of Teacher Education*, *51*(4), 315–27.
Ladd, G.W. (1999). Peer relationships and social competence during early and middle childhood. *Annual Review of Psychology*, *50*(1), 333–59.
La Greca, A.M. and Moore Harrison, H. (2005). Adolescent peer relations, friendships, and romantic relationships: Do they predict social Anxiety and Depression? *Journal of Clinical Child and Adolescent Psychology*, *34*(1), 49–61.
La Guardia, J.G., Ryan, R.M., Couchman, C.E. and Deci, E.L. (2000). Within-person variation in security of attachment: A self-determination theory perspective on attachment, need fulfillment, and well-being. *Journal of Personality and Social Psychology*, *79*(3), 367–84.
Lauder, H. (2009). Policy and governance, introduction. In H. Daniels, H. Lauder and J. Porter (eds), *Knowledge, Values, and Educational Policy: A Critical Perspective.* London: Routledge.
Lipman, P. (2004). *High-Stakes Education: Inequality, Globalization and Urban School Reform.* New York: Routledge.

Lorenz, C. (2012). If you're so smart, why are you under surveillance? Universities, neoliberalism, and new public management. *Critical Inquiry*, *38*(3), 599–629.

Louis, W.R., Mavor, K.I., La Macchia, S.T. and Amiot, C.E. (2014). Social justice and psychology: What is, and what should be. *Journal of Theoretical and Philosophical Psychology*, *34*(1), 14–27.

Marsden, S. and Hough, A. (2013). Children shouldn't have best friends, Private school head argues. *The Telegraph*, 1 May 2013. Available at www.telegraph.co.uk/education/educationnews/10031299/Children-shouldnt-have-best-friends-private-school-head-argues.html.

Nichols, S.L. and Berliner, D.C. (2007). *Collateral Damage: How High-Stakes Testing Corrupts America's Schools*. Cambridge, MA: Harvard Education.

Niemiec, C.P., Lynch, M.F., Vansteenkiste, M., Bernstein, J., Deci, E.L. and Ryan, R.M. (2006). The antecedents and consequences of autonomous self-regulation for college: A self-determination theory perspective on socialization. *Journal of Adolescence*, *29*(5), 761–75.

Niemiec, C.P., Ryan, R.M. and Brown, K.W. (2008). The role of awareness and autonomy in quieting the ego: A self-determination theory perspective. In H.A. Wayment and J.J. Bauer (eds), *Transcending Self-interest: Psychological Explorations of the Quiet Ego* (pp. 107–15). Washington, DC: APA Books.

Niemiec, C.P. and Ryan, R.M. (2009). Autonomy, competence, and relatedness in the classroom: Applying self-determination theory to educational practice. *Theory and Research in Education*, *7*(2), 133–44.

Ntoumanis, N. (2001). A Self-Determination Theory Approach to the Understanding of Motivation in Physical Education. *British Journal of Educational Psychology*, *71*(2), 225–42.

Parker, J.G. and Gottman, J.M. (1989). Social and emotional development in a relational context: friendship interaction from early childhood to adolescence. In T.J. Berndt and G.W. Ladd (eds), *Peer Relationships in Child Development* (pp. 95–131). New York: Wiley.

Patrick, F. (2013). Neoliberalism, the knowledge economy, and the learner: Challenging the inevitability of the commodified self as an outcome of education. *International Scholarly Research Network: Education*, *2013*, 8.

Pelletier, L.G., Séguin-Lévesque, C. and Legault, L. (2002). Pressure from above and pressure from below as determinants of teachers' motivation and teaching behaviors. *Journal of Educational Psychology*, *94*(1), 186–96.

Polanyi, K. (1944). *The Great Transformation: The Political and Economic Origins of Our Time*. Boston: Beacon Press.

Prilleltensky, I. (2008). The role of power in wellness, oppression, and liberation: The promise of psychopolitical validity. *Journal of Community Psychology*, *36*, 116–36.

Robertson, S. (2007). 'Remaking the World': Neo-liberalism and the transformation of education and teachers' labour. In L. Weis and M. Compton (eds), *The Global Assault on Teachers, Teaching and their Unions*. New York: Palgrave.

Rogers, C. (1959). Significant learning: In therapy and in education. *Educational Leadership*, *16*(3), 232–42.

Rogers, M. and Tannock, T., (2013). Are classrooms meeting the psychological needs of children with ADHD symptoms? A Self-Determination Theory perspective. *Journal of Attention Disorders*, Online First, 2013.

Roth, G., Assor, A., Kanat-Maymon, Y. and Kaplan, H. (2007). Autonomous motivation for teaching: How self-determined teaching may lead to self-determined learning. *Journal of Educational Psychology*, *99*(4), 761–74.

Rustin, S. (2011). The Saturday Interview: Mossbourne Academy's Sir Michael Wilshaw. *The Guardian*, 17 September 2011. Available at www.theguardian.com/theguardian/2011/sep/17/Michael-wilshaw-interview [Accessed 11 January 2015].

Ryan, R.M. and Brown, K.W. (2005). Legislating competence: The motivational impact of high-stakes testing as an educational reform. In C. Dweck and A. Elliot (eds), *Handbook of Competence*. New York: Guilford Press.

Ryan, R.M. and Deci, E.L. (2000). Self-determination theory and the facilitation of Intrinsic motivation, social development, and well-being. *American Psychologist*, 55(1), 68–78.

Ryan, R.M. and Deci, E.L. (2004). Overview of self-determination theory: An organismic dialectical perspective. In E.L. Deci and R.M. Ryan (eds), *Handbook of Self-Determination Research* (Ch. 1). Rochester, NY: University of Rochester Press.

Ryan., R.M. and Deci, E.L. (2006). Self-determination and the problem of human autonomy: Does psychology need choice, self-determination and will? *Journal of Personality*, 74(6), 1557–86.

Ryan, R.M. and Deci, E.L. (2007). Self-determination theory and the promotion and maintenance of sport, exercise, and health. In M. Hagger and S. Chatzisarantis (eds), *Intrinsic Motivation and Self-Determination in Exercise and Sport* (Ch. 1). Champaign, IL: Human Kinetics.

Ryan, R.M. and Weinstein, N. (2009). A self-determination theory perspective on high-stakes testing. *Theory and Research in Education*, 7(2), 224–33.

Ryan, R.M., Deci, E.L., Grolnick, W.S. and La Guardia, J.G. (2006). The significance of autonomy and autonomy support in psychological development and psychopathology. In D. Cicchetti and D. Cohen (eds), *Developmental Psychopathology: Vol. 1: Theory and Methods* (2nd edn, pp. 795–849). New York: Wiley.

Ryan, R.M., La Guardia, J.G., Solky-Butzel, J., Chirkov, V. and Kim, Y. (2005). On the interpersonal regulation of emotions: Emotional reliance across gender, relationships, and cultures. *Personal Relationships*, 12(1), 145–63.

Sahlberg, P. (2011). Lessons from Finland. *American Educator*, 35, 32–36.

Sahlberg, P. (2015). Finland's school reforms won't scrap subjects altogether. *The Conversation*, 25 March 2015. Available at https://theconversation.com/finlands-school-reforms-wont-scrap-subjects-altogether-39328.

Shaver, P.R. and Mikulincer, M. (2002). Attachment-related psychodynamics. *Attachment and Human Development*, 4(2), 133–61.

Skinner, B.F. (1953) *Science and Human Behavior*. New York: Macmillan.

Sonu, D. (2012). Illusions of compliance: Performing the public and hidden transcripts of social justice education in neoliberal times, *Curriculum Inquiry*, 42(2), 240–59.

Sullivan, H. (1940). *Conceptions of Modern Psychiatry*. New York: Norton.

Taylor, G., Jungert, T., Mageau, G., Schattke, K., Dedic, H., Rosenfield, S. and Koestner, R. (2014). A Self-Determination Theory Approach to Predicting School Achievement Over Time: The Unique Role of Intrinsic Motivation. *Contemporary Educational Psychology*, 39(4), 342–58.

Timimi, S. (2002). *Pathological Child Psychiatry and the Medicalization Of Childhood*. London, UK: Brunner-Routledge.

Timimi, S. (2005). Naughty boys: Anti-social behaviour, ADHD, and the role of culture. Basingstoke, UK: Palgrave Macmillan.

Timimi, S. and Leo, J. (eds). (2009). *Rethinking ADHD: From Brain to Culture*. Basingstoke, UK: Palgrave Macmillan.

Timimi, S. and Radcliffe, N. (2005). The rise and rise of attention deficit hyperactivity disorder. *Journal of Public Mental Health*, 4(2), 9–13.

Trinke, S.J. and Bartholomew, K. (1997). Hierarchies of attachment relationships in young adulthood. *Journal of Social and Personal Relationships*, 14, 603–25.

Tsai, Y., Kunter, M., Lüdtke, O., Trautwein, U. and Ryan, R.M. (2008). What makes lessons interesting? The role of situational and individual factors in three school subjects. *Journal of Educational Psychology*, 100(2), 460–72.

Ullrich-French, S. and Cox, A.E. (2009). Using cluster analysis to examine the combinations of motivation regulations of physical education students. *Journal of Sport and Exercise Psychology*, *31*, 358–79.

Utman, C.H. (1997). Performance effects of motivational state: A meta-analysis. *Personality and Social Psychology Review*, *1*(2), 170–82.

Vallerand, R.J. and Losier, G.F. (1999). An integrative analysis of intrinsic and extrinsic motivation in sport. *Journal of Applied Sport Psychology*, *11*(1), 142–69.

Vera, E.M. and Speight, S.L. (2003). Multicultural competence, social justice, and counselling psychology: Expanding our roles. *The Counselling Psychologist*, *31*(3), 253–72.

Waiton, S. (2008). *Amoral Panics: The Politics of Antisocial Behavior*. London: Routledge.

Wang, C.K.J., Chatzisarantis, N.L., Spray, C.M. and Biddle, S.J.H. (2002). Achievement Goal Profiles in School Physical Education: Differences in Self-Determination, Sport Ability Beliefs, and Physical Activity. *British Journal of Educational Psychology*, *72*, 433–45.

White, R.W. (1959). Motivation reconsidered: The concept of competence. *Psychological Review*, *66*(5), 297–333.

Wilkesmann, U. and Schmid, C. (2014). Intrinsic and internalised modes of teaching motivation. *Evidence-based HRM*, *2*(1), 6–27.

Winegard, B. and Winegard, C.J. (2011). The awful revolution: Is neoliberalism a public health risk? *Dissident Voice*. Available at http://dissidentvoice.org/2011/04/the-awful-revolution-is-neoliberalism-a-public-health-risk/ [Accessed January 07, 2014].

Wubbels, T., Brekelmans, M., Den Brok, P., Levy, J., Mainhard, T. and Van Tartwijk, J. (2012). Let's Make Things Better. In T. Wubbels, P. Den Brok, J. Van Tartwijk and J. Levy (eds), *Interpersonal Relationships in Education: An Overview of Contemporary Research* (pp. 225–50). Rotterdam: Sense Publishers.

5
SOME CONCLUDING THOUGHTS

> Time is short and the suffering vast. Resources are limited and we must be accountable to oppressed populations who suffer ... Limited resources mean choices. If we [psychologists] continue to use our limited resources only to ameliorate conditions and to tend to the wounded, who will work to transform the very conditions that create exploitation and distress in the first place?
> (Prilleltensky, 2008, p. 132)

I strongly agree with the sense of urgency conveyed in Prilleltensky's words. An important purpose of this book has been to communicate to readers the extent to which neoliberal educational policy has disrupted social and educational justice. Chapter 1 sketched out the various ways in which neoliberal logic in educational policy is oppressive (Ball, 2003a; Brodie, 2007; Giroux, 2002, 2005; Robertson, 2007). As a consequence of such oppression, schools, universities, teachers, parents, academics, children and young people are changing. Furthermore, as educational psychologists, we should be under no doubt that the nature of the oppression has partly been *psychological*. Of psychological oppression, Bartky (1990, p. 22) noted:

> When we describe a people as oppressed, what we have in mind most often is an oppression that is economic and political in character. However, recent liberation movements, the black liberation movement and the women's movement in particular, have brought to light forms of oppression that are not immediately economic or political. It is possible to be oppressed in ways that need involve neither deprivation, legal inequality, nor economic exploitation; one can be oppressed psychologically. To be psychologically oppressed is to be weighed down in your mind; it is to have a harsh dominion exercised over your self-esteem. The psychologically oppressed become their own oppressors; they come to exercise dominion over their

own self-esteem. Differently put, psychological oppression can be regarded as the 'internalization of intimations of inferiority'.

In the pages of this book, I sought to initiate discussion about the ways in which theories of motivation have the *potential* to offer a language through which we might understand, reveal, investigate and challenge psychological manifestations of social injustice and oppression in education. As neoliberal educational policy (and the cultural and political values it serves) proliferates, it threatens to oppress in a myriad of ways – partly by transforming people's psychological experiences of learning and teaching. When such oppression is conceptualised psychologically, it may be understood through *our* theoretical lenses, using *our* tools, constructs and knowledge. In the context of motivational theory, oppression might be seen to exist (a) where educational policies seem to transform the meaning of success for schools, teachers, pupils and academics into something we know to be incompatible with motivation and well-being; (b) where educational policy creates a platform for learning and teaching that ever more pervasively threatens to undermine the basic psychological needs people require to feel genuinely valued, autonomous and positive about themselves through learning and teaching or (c) where the basic psychological needs and motivational characteristics of particular groups of people are thwarted and undermined by one-size-fits-all approaches to learning and education.

Fowers (2015) has suggested that if we are to truly colonise psychology with a genuine concern for social justice then we *must* begin reflecting upon, re-examining and (eventually) refining our theoretical apparatus and knowledge accordingly. Critical psychologists (Carr and Batlle, 2015; Louis et al., 2014; Sugarman, 2015) have outlined that this does not mean abandoning our existing theoretical frameworks but carefully reconsidering their relationship with social justice – particularly in the context of neoliberal society. In this book, I have sought simply to stimulate initial debate around the following important questions that concern the interface between motivational science and neoliberal educational policy:

1. What might the knowledge base of a science of educational motivation look like if it were primarily guided by a concern for social justice?
2. How different would this be from the knowledge base that currently exists?
3. What particular issues of injustice would we focus upon and why?
4. How might our dominant theories be mobilised and utilised towards the end of a more just education system?
5. What sorts of research questions might we ask and why would we ask them?
6. How might we reconsider and further develop our key existing theoretical constructs in light of social justice concerns?
7. To date, how has the development of our theories contributed to issues of oppression and injustice that threaten contemporary education?
8. Have we ever unwittingly or inadvertently been complacent about or contributed to oppression?

I am by no means claiming to have answered these questions. Like Fowers (2015), I firmly believe that their consideration will demand much time and significant effort. Nonetheless, I strongly believe it is time we developed space for them and this book is a call to action. I sought simply to provoke consideration of the need for an alternative, more critical space in relation to the psychological frameworks I am familiar with. In the following pages, I would offer some important thoughts for consideration as we proceed with the discussion.

Are we a science of 'the oppressed' or of 'the oppressors'?

Prilleltensky's (2008) comprehensive discussion of power is a reminder that power is not always synonymous with coercion – we must remember that power can operate in subtle and covert ways. For example, as Foucault (1996, 2008) identified, people can be brought to regulate themselves by internalising cultural prescriptions and 'what may seem on the surface as freedom may be questioned as a form of acquiescence whereby citizens restrict their life choices to coincide with a narrow range of socially sanctioned options' (Prilleltensky, 2008, p. 120). As Rose (1999, p. 88) noted:

> Disciplinary techniques and moralizing injunctions as to health, hygiene, and civility are no longer required; the project of responsible citizenship has been fused with individuals' projects for themselves. What began as a social norm here ends as a personal desire. Individuals act upon themselves and their families in terms of the languages, values, and techniques made available to them by professions, disseminated through the apparatuses of the mass media, or sought out by the troubled through the market. Thus, in a very significant sense, it has become possible to govern without governing society – to govern through the 'responsibilized' and 'educated' anxieties and aspirations of individuals and their families.

A key feature of neoliberal power has been the idea that individuals are subtly seduced, persuaded and prompted to cultivate the characteristics thought to be correlated with an active pursuit of a cultural or political prescription. What is more, such persuasion relies heavily upon structural discourse that rewards, rationalises and idealises these prescriptions (Gorz, 1999).

What does this mean, then, in relation to motivational psychology in the context of education? On the one hand, we might consider that striving to ensure that classrooms are filled with genuinely enthused, motivated, hardworking young people is a desirable goal for contemporary schools and for the science of educational motivation. However, as Prilleltensky (2008) has noted, imagine if we were to make this our objective *without* due consideration for the social and political systems in which individuals and schools are nested. It is possible that in our efforts to calibrate and manage individuals' psychological characteristics towards active pursuit of a dominant cultural prescription we might simultaneously dampen their/our need (or desire) to challenge and interrogate the dominant power structures reflected in such cultural prescription. Perhaps, then, our science would serve simply to *depoliticise* oppression by ensuring that individuals become 'happily docile'; psychologically internalising the desire to pursue externally oppressive forces and/or goals.

In relation to power, if our schools, as they currently stand, *were* filled with motivated, engaged and industrious students, would this be sufficient evidence to claim that such children and their teachers were not *still* servants (albeit more *willing* servants) of the same social, cultural and political agenda? Furthermore, would a psychological science that had served to *help construct* their subjectivities as enthusiastic, motivated, willing and compliant students (without attending to the structural and political system) have fundamentally robbed them of *power* – the power to *resist oppression* and *pursue liberation* (Prilleltensky, 2008)? Put differently, wouldn't motivational science have become '*the science of working out ways to make people want to do what those with power want them to want to do*'? Under such circumstances, how *just* would motivational psychology's use of its own power, privilege, expertise and capital be? Would it have been utilised to help liberate those who are oppressed, or to help their oppressors to oppress them? As Prilleltensky (2008, p. 126) has pointed out:

> A warning is called for: It is entirely possible to venture into the community, into schools, and even into government, and to be welcomed with open arms to institute programs and policies that concentrate on changing individuals and not structures. This has, in fact, occurred with many preventive interventions, that even though took place in community settings, were devised to change individual behavior, and not structures of oppression or domination.

I contend that it is of vital importance for motivational psychologists to (at least) be mindful of this critical issue and give it due consideration. Critiquing, objecting to and resisting oppressive educational structures is as worthy (if not *more* worthy) a goal as focusing upon changing individual behaviour *within* oppressive structural parameters.

Prilleltensky's 'psychopolitical validity'

How might we proceed in relation to research and practice agendas that wish to place issues of social justice, oppression and liberation at the forefront of inquiry? For Prilleltensky (2008, p. 129), 'it is only when we achieve an integrated political and psychological understanding of power, wellness, and oppression that we can effectively change the world around us'. To this end, Prilleltensky (2008) has coined the notion of psychopolitical validity. Psychopolitical validity is a helpful starting point, whether we wish (a) simply to employ the notion as something that reminds us of the importance of considering psychology's relationship to politics, oppression and liberation or (b) to adopt it as a more formal measure of validity, alongside other measures that are routinely employed to make judgements and decisions about quality and worthiness of research or interventions.

The central aim of psychopolitical validity for Prilleltensky (2008) is to ensure that psychology and the social sciences demonstrate awareness of the role of power in relation to wellness, oppression and liberation. *Wellness* stems from the simultaneous, balanced and contextually sensitive satisfaction of personal, relational and collective needs. *Personal needs* (e.g. health, self-determination, meaning, spirituality, opportunities for growth) are closely linked to the satisfaction of *collective needs* (e.g. adequate health care, environmental protection, education, welfare policies and a measure of economic equality) in the sense that public resources have a significant impact upon people's ability to pursue aspirations congruent with the self and maintain personal health and wellness. Furthermore, *relational needs* refer to healthy relationships between individuals and groups, reflected in both a respect for diversity and democratic participation. For Prilleltensky (2008, p. 123), 'respect for diversity ensures that people's unique identities are affirmed by others, while democratic participation enables community members to have a say in decisions affecting their lives'.

Psychopolitical validity's concern with *oppression* stems from the assumption that oppression

> entails a state of asymmetric power relations characterized by domination, subordination, and resistance, where the dominating persons or groups exercise their power by the process of restricting access to material resources and imparting in the subordinated persons or groups self-deprecating views about themselves. It is only when the latter can attain a certain degree of conscientization that resistance can begin. (Prilleltensky, 2008, p. 127)

Such asymmetric power relations between various groups and classes of people can lead to suffering, inequality, exploitation, marginalisation and injustice. What is more, as noted earlier, oppression is not simply a political or economic issue. Psychological oppression exists, and sensitivity and concern with it is paramount. Finally, Prilleltensky's (2008) ideas about psychopolitical validity also include the notion of *liberation*. Liberation simply refers to the resistance of oppression. For Prilleltensky (2008, p. 128), 'liberation is a condition in which oppressive forces no longer exert their dominion over a person or a group. Liberation may be from psychological and/or political influences ... there is rarely political without psychological oppression, and vice versa'.

So, how might psychologists and social scientists evaluate the potential of their research, knowledge and interventions *in relation* to the interconnected ideas of *wellness*, *oppression* and *liberation* that comprise psychopolitical validity? Prilleltensky (2008) has offered a framework that serves as a very useful guide in this respect. The framework asks important questions of researchers in relation to the key features of psychopolitical validity. I list some of these important questions here:

In relation to wellness

- Does our work contribute to institutions that support and seek to nurture emancipation, social justice, peace and human development?
- Does it enhance awareness of the subjective and psychological forces preventing solidarity and identity acceptance?
- Does it contribute to personal and social responsibility and awareness of forces preventing commitment to justice?
- Does it serve to build trust, cohesion and connection in those that support social justice and wish to resist oppression?

In relation to oppression

- Does our work challenge and resist the role of its own reference group in relation to the oppression of others?
- Does it build awareness of the ways in which oppressive forces operate and seek to unmask them?
- Does it seek to contribute to the personal depowerment of oppressors?
- Does it contribute to the struggle against in-group out-group discrimination and marginalisation?

In relation to liberation

- Does it support networks of resistance and social change movements?
- Does it contribute to structural depowerment of oppressors?
- Does it contribute to the struggle to maintain and recover personal and political identities in the face of oppressive forces?
- Does it serve to reduce complacency and collusion within exploitative systems?

(Prilleltensky, 2008, p. 132)

From the discussions relating to the interface between goal theory, self-determination theory and features of neoliberal educational policy in the last two chapters, I would contend that our theoretical frameworks (a) could do much, much more to increase the psychopolitical validity of research and knowledge development, and (yet) (b) nonetheless hold great potential to contribute significantly in relation to resisting oppression and liberation.

Increasing psychopolitical validity

My intention in this book has been to stimulate discussion, debate and movement towards a critical space in motivational theory that genuinely stems from prioritising issues such as social justice, oppression and liberation. It has not been my intention to sketch out a precise agenda for what such a space would look like. Such an endeavour is far beyond the remit of a single book. As Fowers (2015) has noted, it takes time, collective effort and long-term struggle to carve out such a space and this will be an organic process. What is more, my call to consider a critical space in relation to frameworks such as goal theory and SDT in motivational educational psychology is by no means a reflection of the fact that these theories are in any way more or less in need of a critical space than any other framework. As Carr and Batlle (2015) have alluded in the critical psychology literature, most theoretical frameworks have the potential to mobilise and interrogate their knowledge base in relation to the injustices of neoliberal society if they carefully research, reflect and re-examine themselves. Rather, my attempts to interrogate the motivational frameworks explored in this book relate to Fowers' (2015) suggestion that we ought to have an intimate understanding and relationship with the theories we seek to reflect upon and re-examine. In this sense, as a researcher who has spent a decade exploring, researching and appreciating the value in goal theory and SDT, I am simply better placed to critically engage with these particular ideas.

Our knowledge base

I believe Fowers (2015) is right. In a science of educational motivation, it is critical that we interrogate, reflect upon, re-evaluate and continue to develop our knowledge base, *mindful* of social justice, oppression and liberation as they relate to educational policy. As my reflections upon goal theory and SDT have served to highlight, we have built a substantial knowledge base related to personal, collective and relational well-being that has the potential to speak powerfully to assumptions, ideas and practices that underpin neoliberal educational policy. To be mindful of social justice, oppression and liberation, I believe it is vital that we (a) familiarise ourselves with the ways in which educational policy, structures and systems can be considered to be oppressive, to undermine social justice and to thwart well-being; (b) carefully consider our knowledge base, theoretical constructs and assumptions *in relation* to these oppressive political and educational structures, exploring and critiquing the ways in which (1) we might challenge them, (2) we have been complacent about them, or (3) we might have colluded with them (Prilleltensky, 2008) and (c) consider the best ways for our knowledge to develop (in terms of questions, hypotheses, assumptions and constructs) if we are truly to forge a critical space that builds awareness of psychological oppression, unmasks it and seeks to liberate individuals and groups from it. As Louis *et al.* (2014) have noted, only then can our knowledge, tools and expertise better align with social justice.

Who is our knowledge for?

But the above isn't enough. Prilleltensky (2008) has highlighted the fact that psychological knowledge has always been intimately connected to power, whether psychologists have cared to admit it or not:

> When we read histories of psychology, we find countless examples of psychologists' declaration of independence from power (Herman, 1995). They usually come in the form of claims to objectivity and value neutrality, announcing that psychologists study people 'out there' in a manner that is not affected by their own interests and power. No need to rush towards conspiracy theories, however, for many of us were not even aware that power would be so pervasive and invisible at the same time . . . we take it for granted that psychology pursues human welfare in a manner that is always just. (p. 117)

In relation to this, it is critical to consider what we *do* with our knowledge. Who is it for? Why? And how does this relate to power and oppression? Paulo Freire (2000) noted the need to carefully consider the extent to which science, despite its claims toward value neutrality, is frequently a facilitator of oppressive regimes, albeit unwittingly:

> . . . the oppressor, in order to dominate, tries to deter the drive to search, the restlessness, and the creative power which characterize life, it kills life. More and more, the oppressors are using science and technology as unquestionably powerful instruments for their purpose: the maintenance of the oppressive order through manipulation and repression. The oppressed, as objects, as 'things', have no purposes except those their oppressors prescribe for them. (p. 60)

In relation to this, it is worth contemplating Ryan's (2012) recent comments about the psychology of motivation:

> Psychological models of motivation operate on the level of inferred constructs, intended to capture the forces at work in energizing and directing action. Causal models at this level of analysis can be a particularly important point of entry into describing and predicting motivated behaviors. If one wants to intervene in intentional behaviors (e.g., dietary habits, work practices, physical activity and exercise), knowing the types of feedback, meanings, significant cognitions, and perceived social contexts that support or thwart these behaviors provides considerable leverage. (p. 5)

There are important questions for us to reflect upon in relation to this, such as (a) 'considerable leverage' in relation to what, (b) for whom and (c) to what end? Such questions are important in relation to the issues of power, oppression and liberation highlighted by Prilleltensky and Freire. If we do not pay critical attention to the ways in which our knowledge is utilised and employed in relation to power then (a) our knowledge could serve as a useful weapon for those who enforce oppressive policy in the sense that *our knowledge* could (unbeknown to us) be utilised to dampen voices of resistance and maintain the status quo, and (b) we risk compromising psychopolitical validity and our ethical obligations by leaving ourselves open to allegations of complacency and collusion with exploitative systems (Prilleltensky, 2008; Sugarman, 2015).

For example, in Chapter 4, I discussed how goal theorists should critically interrogate and challenge the ways in which the 'language' of goal theory has been pulled into high stakes testing policy. As Allen (2012) argued in the sociological literature, simply transforming the *way in which we go about* monitoring and controlling pupil trajectories in relation to test results (moving from a 'harsher' normative 'ranking system' to a 'softer', mastery-oriented process of 'individual trajectories') may in the end simply be a convenient smokescreen for forces of power seeking to find softer ways of achieving the same controlling end. As such, our theoretical language risks being 'employed' as a motivational facilitator of a mechanism of governance. We must therefore be critical of the ways in which our language and constructs are being employed (e.g. is this *really* a mastery-oriented approach that we would endorse? If so, why? If not, why not? In what ways should we be critical of how policy has borrowed and interpreted our language? How might we challenge it? Why?).

It is critical to consider who our knowledge is constructed *for* in relation to issues of empowerment, oppression and liberation. To this end, Prilleltensky (2008) has suggested that we must attend to the experience of people themselves *before* 'we try to prescribe a dose of either personal or collective wellness' (p. 126). Helping to liberate people from oppressive forces requires us to attend and listen to the ways in which people feel oppressed and where they see potential for avenues of resistance. To this end, far too little recognition has been made by psychologists for the idea that, were we to genuinely prioritise efforts towards liberation and take up the struggle, *we* are not best placed to *be* the liberators. In *Pedagogy of the Oppressed*, Paulo Freire (2000) made a point of underlining this extremely important issue:

> Certain members of the oppressor class join the oppressed in their struggle for liberation, thus moving from one pole of the contradiction to the other. Theirs is a fundamental role, and has been so throughout the history of this struggle. It happens, however, that as they cease to be exploiters or indifferent spectators or simply the heirs of exploitation and move to the side of the exploited, they almost always bring with them the marks of their origin: their prejudices and their deformations, which include a lack of confidence in the people's ability to think, to want, and to know. Our converts truly desire to transform the unjust order; but because of their background they believe that they must be the executors of the transformation. They talk about the people, but they do not trust them; and trusting the people is the indispensable precondition for revolutionary change. A real humanist can be identified more by his trust in the people, which engages him in their struggle, than by a thousand actions in their favor without that trust. (p. 60)

In Chapter 5, I discussed the myriad of ways in which educational policy might be seen to undermine people's basic psychological needs as they are conceptualised in SDT. But what would people *themselves* think and feel if they were privy to the motivational knowledge base provided by theories such as SDT? In light of such knowledge, how would *they* perceive the structural barriers in education that undermine their experiences of basic psychological needs such as competence, autonomy and relatedness? How would they feel about such structural barriers? Empowered with the knowledge our field has generated, what sort of resistance would they choose to engage in and why? Movement towards resisting oppression and liberation perhaps requires us to help conscientise teachers and young people, letting them in on what *we* think we know, seeking to enable and empower *them* with this knowledge and, in light of it, working *with* them against psychological oppression. Perhaps most significantly of all, it is important to recognise that this would also mean, in some senses, relinquishment of *our own* power – as the experts, the authority and the prescribers of solutions to passive recipients.

Walking the talk

It is difficult to contest the fact that most academic researchers in higher education are caught in the same web of oppressive structures as the teachers and young people in education many of us would seek to help liberate. As noted from the discussions in Chapter 2, for many critics (Cribb and Gerwitz, 2013; Giroux, 2002; Patrick, 2013), the last thirty years have witnessed a 'hollowing out' of universities themselves – and of our knowledge. Our institutions (charged to *produce* knowledge) have become 'identified with an economic value system that shapes all reality in its own image' (Brancaleone and O'Brien, 2011, p 502). Accordingly, we must remember that the very definition and value of our knowledge itself is transforming, together with its mode of production and the everyday practices through which it is brought into being. As the organisational systems and structures of academic life are transformed, academics *themselves* transform – and so does the very nature of the knowledge we produce.

As Sugarman (2015) has noted, within such a system we (the *people* in higher education) are pressured towards becoming enterprising, competitive creatures, whose personalities, character and personal attributes ought to align with the dominant value system. As academics, we are no different from the teachers, students and children we might seek to help liberate. We are under increasing pressure to define ourselves (and the knowledge we produce) as a set of assets, skills and attributes to be managed, maintained, developed and treated as ventures in which to invest. As 'enterprising' academics, we come to think of and administer ourselves and the knowledge we produce as economic interests, judged according to a catalogue of management features and indexes of performativity (e.g. satisfaction, worth, productivity, impact, metrics, initiative, effectiveness, skills, goals, risk and networking) to which we are held accountable in relation to a new language of excellence (Saltman, 2000).

As Massey (2000) has noted, for those of us who object to oppressive neoliberal educational policy, perhaps one of our most significant challenges is to 'bring our lived practice more into line with our theorising *about* that practice' (p. 133). Lorenz (2012) has argued that individual faculty members are persuaded more and more towards particular 'ways of producing knowledge' via mechanisms such as individualised contracts and performance-related pay, with no need for explanations as to why management decides what counts as performance. One of our most significant challenges in the pursuit of knowledge that seeks to *resist* oppressive educational policy, to liberate those oppressed by it, and to further social justice, is that we may face uncomfortable challenges *within ourselves*. Pickerill (2008, p. 484) summarises this nicely:

> I only want to be an academic if I get to do 'good', political work. This may mean that I am forever destined to be caught in-between competing demands, or relegated to the margins of the discipline, or both. There is a messiness in bringing passion to an academic job.

Her words raise extremely important questions that we would all do well to contemplate: (a) On a personal level, as individuals and/or groups of researchers, what is the *genuine* purpose of the research and knowledge *we* seek to produce? (b) Why are *we* really doing it? (c) Have *we ourselves* internalised the dominant vocabulary of management and performativity? (d) Do we regard our knowledge contribution, first and foremost, as a means of pursuing individual performance objectives, career trajectories and metric obligations, in the image of the neoliberal educational value structure? (e) What if *we* believe such a value structure to be oppressive and are committed to the pursuit of knowledge that seeks to challenge, expose, resist and liberate people from it – including ourselves? (f) How do we deal with the hypocrisy in seeking to pursue social justice by producing knowledge that *challenges* and *resists* the very essence of the organisational structures within which we are employed to create it? (g) Is this not quintessential hypocrisy? In some ways, it may prove our most challenging task of all to produce knowledge born out of a desire to challenge, resist and liberate from oppressive educational structures when such knowledge will likely be attacking the very principles of the structures within which it is produced. Negotiating the 'values schizophrenia' (Ball, 2003b) and personal discomfort that this might engender will be a significant challenge.

Concluding comments

In one of the most significant attempts to date to change school culture for the better (in a motivational sense), Maehr and Anderman (1993) reflected upon what they saw as our most significant challenges. First, they noted that all school staff must have the *will* to change:

> Our strategy calls for extensive and intensive investment. Administrators cannot be content merely to handle bureaucratic matters. They must have and be able to convey a sense of purpose in what they and the school as a whole are doing. With that, they must examine, reflect on, evaluate, and work toward the change of school-wide policies and practices that define, communicate, create, and embody the purposes of schooling. The school staff determines school culture through how it decides to organize and manage teaching, learning, and school relationships. It is a primary function of administration to be concerned with such organization and management. The staff as a whole also must be involved beyond the confines of defining their own instructional routines. (p. 602)

This, they further argued, means that we must consider the ways in which we can engage and motivate *people* in education to elicit and work towards such change. To this end, one of the most powerful features of change identified was eloquently captured by a teacher in Maehr and Anderman's (1993, p. 602) study, who noted that 'we need to have the same kind of environment that we're trying to give our students'. We must recognise that changing the motivational environment for children will necessitate changing it for teachers and administrators too. They also noted that changing motivational environments so that they are better positioned to offer motivational equality, well-being and optimal learning also requires a *mission*. By this, Maehr and Anderman (1993) were referring to an *idea*, an *idea* of what schools might look like if they were designed to bring about motivational equality in teachers and learners. Our theoretical frameworks and knowledge clearly have much to offer in relation to sketching out this idea and to helping institutions and people map out a pathway towards it.

However, we must also remember that this is a political exercise. We cannot make progress towards what seem to be 'psychologically just' visions of schooling if we are not mindful of the oppressive policy structures to which teaching and learning are currently tethered. We have the power to employ our knowledge to speak to oppressive policy structures, to challenge them and (where necessary) to resist them. We also have the power to work with the oppressed (and given that many of us function within oppressive institutions, we are *among* them) and to employ our knowledge towards liberation and resistance. The extent to which we have done so to date is important to reflect upon and, in the pages of this book, I have sought to initiate the sorts of discussions that might help us to do so.

References

Allen, A. (2012). Cultivating the myopic learner: The shared project of high-stakes and low-stakes assessment. *British Journal of Sociology of Education*, *33*(5), 641–59.

Ball, S. (2003a). Social justice in the head: Are we all libertarians now? In C. Vincent (ed.), *Social Justice, Education, and Identity* (pp. 31–50). London: Routledge Falmer.

Ball, S.J. (2003b). The teacher's soul and the terrors of performativity. *Journal of Educational Policy*, *18*(2), 215–28.

Bartky, S.L. (1990). *Femininity and Domination: Studies in the Phenomenology of Domination*. New York: Routledge.
Brancaleone, D. and O'Brien, S. (2011). Educational commodification and the (economic) sign value of learning outcomes. *British Journal of Sociology of Education*, *32*(4), 501–19.
Brodie, J. (2007). Reforming social justice in neoliberal times. *Studies in Social Justice*, *1*(2), 93–107.
Carr, S. and Batlle, I.C. (2015). Attachment theory, neoliberalism, and social conscience. *Journal of Theoretical and Philosophical Psychology*, 35(3), 160–76.
Cribb, A. and Gewirtz, S. (2013). The hollowed-out university? A critical analysis of changing institutional and academic norms in UK higher education. *Discourse*, *34*(3), 338–50.
Foucault, M. (1996). *Istoria nebuniei în perioada clasică*. Bucuresti: Humanitas.
Foucault, M. (2008). *The Birth of Biopolitics: Lectures at the Collège de France, 1978–1979*, translated by G. Burchell. In A.I. Davidson, (ed.), New York: Palgrave Macmillan.
Fowers, B.J. (2015). The promise of a flourishing theoretical psychology. *Journal of Theoretical and Philosophical Psychology*, 35(3), 145–59.
Freire, P. (2000). *Pedagogy of the Oppressed*. London: Bloomsbury Publishing.
Giroux, H.A. (2002). Neoliberalism, corporate culture, and the promise of higher education: The university as a democratic public sphere. *Harvard Educational Review*, *72*(4), 425–63.
Giroux, H.A. (2005). The Terror of neoliberalism: Rethinking the significance of cultural politics. *College Literature*, *32*(1), 1–19.
Gorz, A. (1999). *Reclaiming Work*. London: Pluto.
Herman, E. (1995). *The Romance of American Psychology: Political Culture in the Age of Experts*. Berkeley, CA: University of California Press.
Lorenz, C. (2012). If you're so smart, why are you under surveillance? Universities, neoliberalism, and new public management. *Critical Inquiry*, *38*(3), 599–629.
Louis, W.R., Mavor, K.I., La Macchia, S.T. and Amiot, C.E. (2014). Social justice and psychology: What is, and what should be. *Journal of Theoretical and Philosophical Psychology*, *34*(1), 14–27.
Maehr, M.L. and Anderman, E.M. (1993). Reinventing schools for early adolescents: Emphasizing task goals. *Elementary School Journal*, *93*(5), 593–610.
Massey, D. (2000). Practising political relevance. *Transactions of the Institute of British Geographers*, *25*(2), 131–33.
Patrick, F. (2013). Neoliberalism, the knowledge economy, and the learner: Challenging the inevitability of the commodified self as an outcome of education. *International Scholarly Research Network: Education*, *2013*, 8.
Pickerill, J. (2008). The surprising sense of hope. *Antipode*, *40*(3), 482–87.
Prilleltensky, I. (2008). The role of power in wellness, oppression and liberation: The promise of psychopolitical validity. *Journal of Community Psychology*, *36*(2), 116–36.
Robertson, S. (2007). 'Remaking the World': Neo-liberalism and the Transformation of Education and Teachers' Labour. In L. Weis and M. Compton (eds), *The Global Assault on Teachers, Teaching and their Unions*. New York: Palgrave.
Rose, N. (1999). *Powers of Freedom: Reframing Political Thought*. New York: Cambridge University Press.
Ryan, R.M. (2012). Motivation, and the organization of human behavior: Three reasons for the reemergence of a field. In R.M. Ryan (ed.), *Oxford Handbook of Human Motivation* (pp. 3–13). Oxford, UK: Oxford University Press.
Sugarman, J. (2015). Neoliberalism and psychological ethics. *Journal of Theoretical and Philosophical Psychology*, *35*(2), 103–16.

INDEX

accountability, culture of 24–25, 28–30
achievement goals 61–64
'adequate yearly academic progress' (AYP) (US) 25
aims-based goals 72
American Psychological Association membership 47
approach goals 62, 66–67, 74
Aristotle 113
arts and humanities, status of 21
attachment theory 100–101, 104
attention deficit hyperactivity disorder (ADHD) 44, 106–107
authenticity 104–105
autonomy: choice and 109–114; circumstantial 110–114; need for 93, 95–96, 104–105, 109–114; of teachers 28, 104–105
avoidance goals 62, 66–67, 74

basic needs theory 92
behaviourism 102
BERA Special Interest Group in Social Justice 3
Birth of Biopolitics, The (Foucault) 30, 39–40
Bourdieu, Pierre 31, 40
buffering hypothesis 64, 78–79
'bullshit' 33
business ontology: in education 18, 42; *see also* market values; quasi-market values

Cameron, David 98
capitalism, knowledge 18–20
care, viewed as a commodity 19
childhood: changed nature of 45–46; commodification of 45–46; limiting friendships 99, 100–101
choice: autonomy and 109–114; increased parental 23; lack of genuine 23
circumstantial autonomy 110–114
classical liberalism 16
Code of Ethics and Conduct (BPA) 39
Code of Ethics for Psychologists (CPA) 39
commodification: of childhood 45–46; of knowledge 42; of learners 30–31
Communism 114
competence, need for 60, 61, 92
competition, neoliberal focus on 16, 40
conditional regard 8, 101
congruence 103–105
control: locus of 95; valued above all else 19; *see also* power
critical psychology *see* psychology

Deconstructing Developmental Psychology (Burman) 43
dehumanising effect of testing 27
discrimination, motivational 105–109

economic growth, education as driver for 18, 26

'economic man' (*Homo Economicus*) 16, 30, 40–41
education *see* higher education; neoliberal education policies; schooling
Educational Binds of Poverty, The (Brown) 107–108
Education Reform Act (1988) 28
Education of Selves: How Psychology Transformed Students (Martin and McLellan) 44
eleven-plus examination 5–6, 8
equality, neoliberalism's failure to deliver 32
Erikson, Erik 113
'Essence of Neoliberalism, The' (Bourdieu) 40
Ethical Principles of Psychologists and Code of Conduct (APA) 39
ethics, psychologists' codes of 39, 47
excellence, regime of 21–22, 43, 76
expenditure on education 32
external regulation 95
extrinsic motivation 94–96

family-work conflict 45
Finnish education system 108–109
'fixed intelligence' 7
'food marketing' 46
Foucault, Michel 8, 16, 30, 39–40, 69–70, 105
'fourth world' 32
Freire, Paulo 7, 19, 113–114, 128, 129
friendships, limiting children's 99, 100–101
fulfillment of potential, equality of 3–4

generativity 113
goal theory: achievement goals 61–64; aims-based goals 72; approach/avoidance 62, 66–67, 74; at crossroads 53, 60; buffering hypothesis 64, 78–79; classroom goal structures 63–64, 78–82; competence 60, 61; dampening effect 63; goal conflict 82; higher order constructs 73–74; and high stakes testing 64–67; mastery goals 61–64, 67–69, 71–73; matching hypothesis 64, 78–79; multiple goal pursuit 62–63, 73–76; overview of 60–64; performance goals 61, 62–64, 65–67; performativity goals 77–78; reasons-based goals 72; switching between goals 63, 74–76; and teachers 78–82
Gove, Michael 98–99

happiness, responsibility for own 41–42
higher education: academic redundancies in 20–21; changing culture of 20–22; market values in 20–22; regime of excellence 21–22, 43, 76; seen as 'means to an end' 22; status of arts and humanities in 21
high stakes testing: goal theory and 64–67; mastery-oriented values in 67–69, 71–73; multiple goals in 73–76; overview of 24–27; performance goals in 65–67; performativity and 77; self-determination theory on 102–105
Homo Economicus 16, 30, 40–41

identified regulation 95
'Importance of Teaching, The' (white paper) 98
inspectorates, private contractors engaged 24
intelligence, 'fixed' 7
internalisation 94–96
intrinsic motivation 66, 93–94
introjected regulation 95, 101
investment in self 41

Journal of Theoretical and Philosophical Psychology 48–49

knowledge: 'hollowing out' of 33, 43; in psychological sciences 43; 'technology' of construction of 42
knowledge capitalism, education and 18–20
'knowledge economy' 18

league tables 24, 25, 68
learner, commodified 30–31
liberalism *see* classical liberalism; neoliberalism
locus of control 93, 95

'McDonaldization of Childhood, The' (Timimi) 45

market values: education reconstructed for 1; *see also* business ontology; quasi-market values
mastery goals 61–64, 67–69, 71–73
matching hypothesis 64, 78–79
'means to an end': higher education seen as 22; schooling seen as 26
'medicalisation of childhood' 10, 44, 106–107
'militant' approach to education 98–99
Miller, David 2–3
minority groups (in psychology) 47–48
'Motivation and Equality' (Nicholls and Burton) 3–4
motivation theory: external regulation 95; extrinsic motivation 94–96; identified regulation 95; integrated regulation 95; intrinsic motivation 66, 93–94; introjected regulation 95, 101; locus of control 95; performativity 77; pluralism (motivational discrimination) 105–109; role of 51–53; *see also* goal theory; self-determination theory
multiple goal pursuit 62–63, 73–76

needs: autonomy 93, 95–96, 104–105, 109–114; basic needs theory 92; competence 60, 61, 92; overlooked by neoliberal education policies 97–101; relatedness 8, 93, 100–101, 104
neoliberal education policies: controlling 97–99; evidence for benefits of 32; high stakes testing as part of 26; one-size-fits-all approach 105–109; psychological critique of 99–101; psychologists complicit in 44, 59, 69–71, 127–131; resistance to 112–113, 130–131; self-determination theory and 97–109
neoliberalism: definitions of 15–17, 31–33; 'programming' of individual 70; role of the state and 16–17, 30
No Child Left Behind (NCLB) Act 25, 26

Office for Standards in Education (OFSTED): engages private contractors 24; teachers' accountability to 28, 29–30
one-size-fits-all approach 107–108

oppression: psychological 6–7, 121–124; psychopolitical validity and 125, 126

'parenting' industry 46
Pedagogy of the Oppressed, The (Freire) 129
performance goals 61, 62–64, 65–67
performance tables 24, 25, 68
performativity: culture of 29–30, 76–77, 81; goals 77–78; motivation 77
personality, and market-based identities 41
policy *see* neoliberal education policies
positive psychology movement 41–42
potential, equality of fulfillment of 3–4
poverty: neoliberalism rationalisation of 17, 32; and one-size-fits-all approach 107–108; test results and 26
power: psychology's relationship with 127–131; utilisation of own 8–9; *see also* control
prescriptions, dominant 70, 123–124
Prilleltensky, Isaac 121, 124–129
psychological oppression 6–7, 121–124
psychology: blind spots in 50; colonisation by new voices 48, 49–50, 122, 130–131; complicit in government policy 44, 59, 69–71, 127–131; critique of neoliberal education policies 99–101; developing critical voice 49–51; lack of critical conscience in 9–11, 39, 43–44, 46–51; minority groups within 47–48; morality in 47; personality types 41; positive psychology movement 41–42; pressure of 'academic entrepreneurship' 43; psychopolitical validity 124–131; quantification of the individual 42
psychopolitical validity 124–131

Qualifications and Curriculum Authority (QCA) 28
quality of teaching, test results and 26
quasi-market values, in schooling 22–24

Rawls, John 1–2
'realness' (of teachers) 103–105
reasons-based goals 72
redundancies, academic 20–21
regime of excellence 21–22, 43, 76
regulation (self-determination theory) 95

relatedness, need for 8, 93, 100–101, 104
resistance, to neoliberal education policies 112–113, 130–131
Rogers, Carl 101, 103–104

SATs 25
schooling: culture of accountability in 24–25, 28–30; league tables 24, 25, 68; parental choice 23; quasi-market values in 22–24; seen as a 'means to an end' 22; as self-perpetuating oligarchy 23–24; 'Special Measures' 28–29
school inspectorates, private contractors engaged 24
self, investment in 41
self-determination theory: and ADHD 107; autonomy 93, 95–96, 104–105, 109–114; competence 92; controlling neoliberal education policies 97–99; and education 92–96; extrinsic motivation 94–96; framework in HE study 54; and high stakes testing 102–105; internalisation 94–96; intrinsic motivation 66, 93–94; and neoliberal education policy 97–109; overview of 92; on pluralism 105–109; regulation 95; relatedness 8, 93, 100–101, 104; teacher autonomy 104–105
self-perpetuating oligarchies (schools as) 23–24
social justice: BERA Special Interest Group in 3; Miller's theory 2–3; neoliberalism disruption of 3; psychology's lack of attention to 9–11, 39, 43–44, 46–51; Rawls' theory 1–2; self-interest and 2–3
Society for the Psychological Study of Social Issues 47
socioeconomic status *see* poverty
'Special Measures' 28–29
state: markets created by 23, 30, 31–32, 40; role of 16–17, 30

Task Group on Assessment and Testing (TGAT) 25, 68
teacher-led assessment 25, 26
teachers: autonomy of 28, 104–105; discourse employed by 79–80; goal theory and 78–82; monitoring of 28; 'performativity' required of 29–30, 76–77, 81; 'realness' of 103–105
Teacher Training Agency (TTA) 28
teaching quality, test results and 26
'teaching to the test' 27
'technology', knowledge construction as a 42
testing: 'adequate yearly academic progress' (AYP) (US) 25; dehumanising effect of 27; eleven-plus examination 5–6, 8; league tables 24, 25, 68; and quality of teaching 26; SATs 25; and socioeconomic status 26; Task Group on Assessment and Testing (TGAT) 25, 68; teacher-led assessment 25, 26; 'teaching to the test' 27; *see also* high stakes testing
Testing Teachers (Jeffrey and Woods) 29
Thatcher, Margaret 17
'troops to teachers' programme 98–99

unconditional positive regard 101
universities *see* higher education

validity, psychopolitical 124–131
value-added models 68–69
voice, developing a critical 49–51

welfare state 17
Wilshaw, Michael 98
work-family conflict 45
workplace, competition in 40

young people, society's commitment to 18